The Way of Thomas

Other books by John R. Mabry

Noticing the Divine: An Introduction to
Interfaith Spiritual Guidance

Faith Styles: Ways People Believe

I Believe in a God Who Is Growing: Process Perspectives
on the Creed, the Sacraments, and the Christian Life

God Has One Eye: The Mystics of the World's Religions

Who Are the Independent Catholics? (with John P. Plummer)

God is a Great Underground River

Crisis and Communion: The Re-Mythologization of the Eucharist

Heretics, Mystics & Misfits

God As Nature Sees God: A Christian Reading of the Tao Te Ching

The Tao Te Ching: A New Translation

The Little Book of the Tao Te Ching

The Way of Thomas

NINE INSIGHTS FOR ENLIGHTENED LIVING FROM THE SECRET SAYINGS OF JESUS

John R. Mabry

BOOKS

Winchester, U.K.
New York, U.S.A.

First published by O Books, 2007
O Books is an imprint of John Hunt Publishing Ltd.,
The Bothy, Deershot Lodge, Park Lane, Ropley, Hants, SO24 0BE, UK
office1@o-books.net
www.o-books.net

Distribution in:

UK and Europe
Orca Book Services
orders@orcabookservices.co.uk
Tel: 01202 665432
Fax: 01202 666219 Int. code (44)

USA and Canada
NBN
custserv@nbnbooks.com
Tel: 1 800 462 6420
Fax: 1 800 338 4550

Australia and New Zealand
Brumby Books
sales@brumbybooks.com
Tel: 61 3 9761 5535
Fax: 61 3 9761 7095

Far East (offices in Singapore, Thailand,
Hong Kong, Taiwan)
Pansing Distribution Pte Ltd
kemal@pansing.com
Tel: 65 6319 9939
Fax: 65 6462 5761

South Africa
Alternative Books
altbook@peterhyde.co.za
Tel: 021 447 5300
Fax: 021 447 1430

Text copyright John R. Mabry 2007

Design: Jim Weaver

ISBN-13: 978 1 84694 030 9
ISBN-10: 1 84694 030 3

A CIP catalogue record for this book is available from the British Library.

Printed in the US by Maple Vail

Portions of chapter eight were originally printed in
Creation Spirituality magazine, Spring, 1995.

This book is dedicated to
FLAVIO EPSTEIN

who first taught me about the way of the twin

Contents

Introduction: The story of the Gospel of Thomas

Nell appeared at our church looking like a cat caught in the headlights. A couple of times she looked like she was ready to jump out of her skin, so I took care not to surprise her. At coffee hour after the service she asked if she could speak to me privately, so I showed her into my office and asked what I could do.

"I don't know why I'm here," she confided. "I don't believe any of this Jesus stuff anyway."

I asked her exactly which "Jesus stuff" she was referring to.

"You know," she said, "miracles, and that stuff about dying for our sins and rising from the dead. And all the politics of the church – what they've turned him into. It makes me want to gag. I mean, I love Jesus, I love what he taught, what he stood for – but what they've done to him? No thanks."

I smiled and nodded, "You and me both." She looked surprised. I leaned in and, in a conspiratorial whisper, said, "What if I told you that scholars now have in their possession sayings of Jesus which have been kept secret for almost fifteen hundred years – sayings which comprise the earliest and most reliable gospel we know of, and that in it there is not a single mention of a miracle. Not only that, but there is no mention of either a crucifixion or a resurrection?"

"I'd say you were pulling my leg," she breathed, enthralled.

"Have you ever read *The Gospel of Thomas*...?"

Nell is not alone. I have heard nearly identical objections from many people at our church and amongst my students. I myself have struggled with the version of Jesus "sold" by the institutional church. For years I have asked myself, how can I follow Jesus with integrity when it does not seem like the Jesus I have been given by my tradition has any? How can I entrust myself to a tradition I simply do not trust?

Many of us are searching for a trustworthy Jesus, one that does not insult us, treat us as children, or enslave us. We want to know how to save our souls without selling them, but that is no easy task. We are suspicious of the institutional churches which often seem to put political realities before human compassion, and the imperial Jesus they offer just rings false.

The Gospel of Thomas is not an authoritative cure for the disinformation proffered by the traditions we have inherited, but it certainly does provide food for thought and a much-needed corrective lens. It does not give us an unmediated view of the historical Jesus nor offer his unfiltered teachings, but it does get us closer to the source than we have been before, and what it reveals is not only surprising but strangely relevant to our contemporary dilemmas of faith. It is, it seems, a Gospel amazingly suited to our times, and yet it was very nearly lost to the sands of time altogether.

In this book we will explore nine insights central to this unique and revolutionary Gospel. These insights can revolutionize the way we see not only Jesus, but ourselves, each other, and the universe. They offer us not a new religion, but the very opposite of religion: a living spirituality dependent not upon any church or dogma, but upon the unmediated experience of mystical union common to all true spiritualities.

What is the origin of this amazing document? Where did it come from? What were the ancient communities that revered Jesus' secret sayings, and what did they teach? And, more importantly, what does any of this have to offer us today?

The story of the Gospel of Thomas

The Gospel of Thomas is an ancient collection of sayings attributed to Jesus that records the memory and teachings of a very early school of Christianity, the Thomas school. According to their tradition, the founders of the Thomas school were members of Jesus' own family, and therefore, presumably very close to the source. The story of this gospel is really the story of the community of Jesus' earliest followers and the peculiar spirituality they proclaimed to be Jesus' own.

The complex history of Christianity begins with one man, Jesus. He was an itinerant rabbi, probably a Pharisee, who – most scholars agree – never intended to start a new religion. He was instead a reformer who attacked the hypocrisy he saw in his co-religionists, taught a radical egalitarianism, and tried to redirect his pupils' apocalyptic focus from the future to the here-and-now (see Crossan, 54–74). According to most accounts, he so threatened the religious and political power structures of his day that he was captured, tried, and executed as a criminal. For most movements, this would be the end of the story, but there was something different about Jesus from the very beginning – something his followers sensed, and that compelled them to leave family and security behind to follow him.

After his death, his disciples experienced an intense period of grief. Eventually they came to feel that Jesus was present with them once again and in their midst in a mystical way that they could not quite comprehend or articulate.

There were, at this point, still no "Christians" as we think of them today. Jesus' followers continued to practice their native faith, Judaism, and continued to think of themselves as Jews, worshipping in the temple, and holding positions of responsibility in the synagogues (Acts 2:46–47). In the Gospel of Thomas, Jesus' disciples ask him, "We know that you will leave us. Who will step up, who will lead us?" Jesus answered them, "Wherever you come from, you should go to James the righteous, for whom heaven and earth came into being."

He was speaking of his brother, James. It was common in ancient times for the family business to pass to the nearest relative, and this was as true of religious movements as it was political dynasties or property (think of the claim of the Shi'ite Muslims, for example, that Mohammad's authority should pass to his kin). Upon Jesus' death, leadership did indeed pass to James, even though there is no evidence that his brother was a follower of his during his life. The largest community of followers was based in Jerusalem, and James proved to be a solid, if unimaginative leader. The biblical epistle of James is probably his work, and with its emphasis on obedience to the law and the importance of compassionate action it betrays many signs of what would become Jewish Christian theology.

Jewish Christian Sources. For the past 2000 years, most people have derived their knowledge about the church's early life from the biblical New Testament accounts. But as we shall see, these writings are highly polemic, and do not represent the memory of the Jewish Christians, the original followers of Jesus. Fortunately, many writings do survive that have helped scholars piece together the teachings of the early Jesus Community. Many Jewish Christian sources are preserved in a collection now called the *Psuedo-Clementines* (as they were falsely attributed to a writer named Clement). Many layers of text representing the views of Christian groups that disagreed with the Jewish Christians have been added to these writings, but the interpolations are fairly easy for scholars to identify, and much of the original text is clearly visible to the careful reader. These writings contain a lengthy history of salvation, some letters (two of which are written to James), a highly entertaining early novel (the Clementine "romance") and a collection of sermons that may have been written by Peter himself.

One sect of Jewish Christianity was the Thomas School, with which we are primarily concerned here. Their writings include the *Gospel of Thomas, the Book of Thomas the Contender,* and the *Acts of Thomas.* Also helpful in sorting out the beliefs of this community are the writings of those who were trying to denounce the Jewish Christians as heretics, such as Eusebius. Ironically, in chronicling the Jewish Christians' many theological "errors," the writings of these heresiologists in fact quite helpfully have preserved for us many of the Jewish Christians' teachings and even some sources that have since been lost to us.

The Teachings of the Jewish Christians. James and the community he led held fiercely to the Law of Moses, every bit as fiercely as the Pharisaical movement, of which they were an offshoot. They did not believe that Jesus' teachings had superceded that Law; on the contrary, Jesus had supported it, clarified it, cherished it, and taught them to do the same. They taught nothing that was heretical to Judaism – but they did challenge the local power structures and the authority of the Pharisees and Sadducees, much as Jesus had done, which seemed like heresy to many who confused the Law with the structures that upheld it.

In their teaching, Jesus was simply their rabbi. Their writings contain no mention of a virgin birth story and claimed no supernatural status for Jesus at all. He was, in their eyes, a great prophet, so great that he was the equal – perhaps even the superior – of Moses, and came to complete the Law that Moses had delivered in part. He was not born the messiah, but was granted that privilege because of his unwavering devotion to – and complete understanding of – the Law.

According to the writings of later Jewish Christians, when Moses led the children of Israel out of Egypt, God demanded that they put a stop to the abominable practice of animal sacrifice. Moses interceded, however, and insisted that sacrifice was the only way his people knew how to worship. He begged God not to take it away from them, and suggested a temporary compromise: "permit them to sacrifice, but only to you!" (Schoeps, 82).

God agreed that it was an acceptable compromise for the time being, and instituted very strict instructions for how it was to happen (which we find in the biblical book of Leviticus and sprinkled elsewhere amongst the Torah). But an end to sacrifice was coming. For Jewish Christians, Jesus was the new Moses that was to complete Moses' mission, and put an end to the animal sacrifices God found so repellent. Later Jewish Christians even became vegetarians to further end the needless slaughter of animals.

In addition to ending the temple sacrifices, Jesus challenged the apocalyptic anticipation of the Kingdom of God. The Jews at the time looked forward to the time when the messiah – the anointed one who would be the king – would lead a political revolt, defeat the Roman empire, and set up a theocratic government in Jerusalem. Eventually all the world would bow to this messiah, and the Kingdom of God would finally arrive on earth.

Many people looked to Jesus to be that messiah, but he never claimed such a throne for himself, and instead insisted that the Kingdom of God was not a political reality that would someday arrive, but a spiritual reality that was already present. The Jewish Christians continued this teaching, some of which has come down to us in the teachings of Thomas.

The Trial of James. James, by all accounts, led the Jerusalem community well. His defining moment came late in his life, when he was called before the Sanhedrin, the Jewish high court – the same court that had condemned his brother. James' community – those Jews who continued to follow the teachings of their rabbi, Jesus – was an annoyance to the religious establishment. The court asked James to make a case for their school of thought, "for there should not be two Judaisms, but one" (*Clementine Recognitions* 1:44).

James made an impassioned reply that recalled the entire history of the salvation of the Jewish people. This speech survives in two sources, the Jewish Christians' own writings, and the more familiar Book of Acts, where it is placed in the mouth of Stephen at his martyrdom. Though he was eloquent and passionate, James' rhetoric enflamed the court, and so angered one observer that he threw James down the stairs and nearly killed him (*Clementine Recognitions* 1:70). The attacker was "the man of sin" as the Jewish Christians called him. We know him today as Saul of Tarsus – the apostle Paul.

The Pauline school

It is Paul's school which eventually became the dominant form of Christianity. According to the biblical book of Acts, he was originally known as Saul. He believed the Jewish Christians to be dangerous heretics, and sought to purge Judaism of their numbers. When a crowd arose to stone one Jewish Christian, Stephen (Acts 7), the New Testament says that Saul held their coats and consented to the execution. The Book of Acts further relates, "And on that day a great persecution arose against the church in Jerusalem...but Saul was ravaging the church, and entering house after house, he dragged off men and women and committed them to prison" (Acts 8). (As we have already noted, this differs from the Jewish Christian account, in which it was James, the brother of Jesus and leader of the Jerusalem church, whom Saul tried to kill. Probably the Pauline school substituted Stephen in this account because trying to kill Jesus' brother was simply too inflammatory.)

Then an unforeseen and amazing thing happened to Paul. According to the Book of Acts, he was riding to Damascus when he was struck from his horse by a blinding light. A voice came from the heavens, saying, "Saul, Saul, why do you persecute me?"

"Who are you?" Saul asked the voice.

"I am Jesus, whom you are persecuting." The vision had a profound effect on Saul, and suddenly, many disparate ideas coalesced to form an amazing theological synthesis which was to have great appeal in the non-Jewish world.

According to scholar Hyam Maccoby, Paul's great insight was to wed three disparate elements into one more-or-less coherent system: the history of the Jewish people (and therefore the ability to appropriate the literary legacy of the Jewish scriptures); the story of Jesus the rabbi that had so troubled him; and the Gnostic myth of the savior-come-down-from-heaven *in vogue* in many circles.

Gnosticism was a very important movement at this time, and there were few religions untouched by its philosophy. Though the mythology changes with each religion, there are certain elements which are common to most forms: 1) there is a high god alien to this universe, in which human beings have their source, and to which they long to return; 2) this world is the creation of a flawed or even evil demiurge (a lesser deity), and thus is a place of suffering; 3) humans are saved from this hard world by knowledge of their true plight and the information needed to escape it; 4) a savior comes as an emissary from the alien high god to the world of suffering to deliver this saving knowledge.

In Jewish Gnosticism of the time, the savior was known as Seth, but for Paul and later Christian Gnostics, Jesus was an even better fit. Paul's system appropriates every element of the Gnostic schema with one exception: the world is still the creation of the high god, it is simply ruled over by Satan, whom Paul calls "the god of this world" (2 Corinthians 4:4), and who is, in every other sense, identical to the Gnostic demiurge.

It is not fair to assume that Paul sat around trying to invent this system in order to start a new religion. More likely, in that flash of insight on the road to Damascus, these pieces suddenly fit together in his imagination with the force of a revelation.

Unfortunately, the Gnostic mythological elements in Paul's system were utterly foreign to the Jewish Christians' understanding of their own faith. Soon they began to hear that this man Paul, who formerly had persecuted them, was now preaching about Jesus to Jews and Gentiles alike outside of Israel.

This no doubt caused them some confusion, but they were doubly perplexed when they encountered the content of his teaching. He was telling Gentiles that they did not have to become Jews to follow Jesus, and was preaching that Jesus was a divine being come into this world as a savior. He also said that those in Jerusalem did not properly understand Jesus and his mission (Acts 13:27), and declared himself to be the equal of the apostles (the twelve disciples specifically chosen by Jesus), and in fact, claimed that title for himself.

The Jewish Christians were outraged, and called him "Paul the Apostate" rather than "Paul the Apostle." The Jewish Christian writings at every turn repudiate his teaching. Paul frequently tried to raise money to send to the Jerusalem church, perhaps trying to buy their favor in order to lend his own communities some legitimacy, but his efforts were rebuffed.

Finally, Paul was summoned to Jerusalem to make his case before James. In the account written by Paul's community in the Book of Acts, he is warmly received, and the Jerusalem community "glorified

God" when they heard about his exploits amongst the gentiles (21:20). More likely, the outcry recorded seven verses later is a more accurate description of how he was received: "Men of Israel, help! This is the man who is teaching men everywhere against the people and the law.... Moreover he also brought [gentiles] into the temple, and he has defiled the holy place."

According to this account, James ruled that Gentiles do not have to be circumcised or convert to Judaism to follow Jesus. If James did make such a ruling, then he surely sealed the fate of the Jewish Christian community; for it was to be Paul's version of the Jesus story that would be eagerly received in every corner of the ancient world.

There continued to be much tension between the two communities for many years. This tension is evident in the Pauline writings (the New Testament), but for the most part the disagreements have been smoothed over in these accounts, providing the illusion of a contiguous community in unbroken communion from Jesus himself to Paul's communities. From the Jewish Christian perspective, however, nothing could be further from the truth.

Exile in Syria

The latter half of the first century was a difficult time for the Jewish Christians – indeed for all Jews. In the year 70 CE, the Romans subdued the Judeans with a terrible show of military force. They dissolved the local governments and utterly destroyed the Temple in Jerusalem. The Jewish people scattered, taking with them only what they could carry. This is the beginning of the Jewish Diaspora, and the Jewish Christians were part of it.

The largest group of Jewish Christians settled in Syria, to the north of Israel. There they flourished for a time, and were, in fact, the dominant form of Christianity in the region for several centuries. They continued to see themselves as Jews, but were increasingly unwelcome in the synagogues. Finally, they formed their own synagogues and trained their own rabbis. As the centuries wore on they became increasingly xenophobic, and developed a theology that was even more strict in its adherence to the Mosaic law.

They were the first to develop a system of source criticism regarding scripture, identifying some sections of the Torah as authentic and some as non-authoritative insertions by later – presumably uninspired – scribes. One Jewish Christian group took to calling themselves the *evyonim*, or "the poor," in reference to the ideal of poverty held in their community.

Finally, in the fifth century, the Pauline church set up its first bishop in Syria, and Paul's churches became the dominant form of Christianity in that place, too (Schoeps, 30). Some Jewish Christians most likely re-joined the Jewish community, and some were no doubt absorbed into Pauline Christianity. Only one family of Jewish Christians survived beyond the fourth century – the Thomas school.

The Thomas school

Didymous Judas Thomas is well accounted for in the "official" writings of the Christian church. He is listed among the original twelve apostles, and immortalized in the popular imagination as "doubting Thomas." He may also be the author of the canonical epistle of Jude. When we meet him in the Pauline gospels he is often referred to as "the twin." "Didymous" means "twin" in Greek, just as "Thomas" derives from "twin" in Hebrew (*t'omit*). But since the text does not say *whose* twin it is, why mention that he is a twin at all? Perhaps because it is assumed that the person to whom Thomas is twin is known to all and does not need identifying.

The literature of the Thomas school states quite clearly that Thomas is the twin brother of Jesus himself. *The Book of Thomas the Contender,* and the *Acts of Thomas* both identify Thomas and Jesus as twins. Although the Pauline canon mentions Thomas the Twin, and also lists a "Judas" amongst Jesus' brothers, it does not connect the two. No doubt this is because the memory of Thomas as Jesus' twin had to be jettisoned to make room for the myth of Mary's virginity. Later church teachings went even further, insisting on

Mary's "perpetual" virginity, necessitating further mythologizing to make Jesus' siblings the products of Joseph's previous marriage. The Thomas literature contains no such pretensions.

While the Thomas school shared much in common with their fellow Jewish Christians they cultivated a distrust of authority, and consequently their allegiance to the Mosaic law was tempered by a spiritual individualism unknown to any other school of early Christianity. Unlike other Jewish Christians, they believed Jesus' teachings to be salvific in and of themselves, instead of simply pointing to the source of salvation they had always known, the Torah. The Gospel of Thomas says, "Whoever happens upon the meaning of these words will not taste Death." This Gospel functions similar to a collection of Zen koans. Many of the sayings appear nonsensical on the surface, but meditating upon them can bring one to a shocking shift in perspective which the Thomas school believed brought with it eternal life.

Also unlike most Jewish Christians, the Thomas school was actively evangelistic. Since their theology placed less emphasis on Jewish purity and more on a kind of enlightenment it lent itself to the consideration of non-Jews as well.

According to the memory of the Thomas school, Thomas journeyed to India, where he met great success until he was martyred by an Indian King. In reality, it was probably not Thomas himself who went to India, but later disciples of Thomas' school who actually made the journey.

The Mar Thoma Christians in India trace their beginnings to this early missionary journey. This church was completely independent of Pauline tradition until the fifteenth century, when the Portuguese made the first attempts to colonize India. The Portuguese coerced the Mar Thoma church into compliance with Roman Catholic belief and practice, and burned all of their ancient prayer books and theological writings. Today we are left with precious little evidence regarding the origins, theologies, and liturgies of the Mar Thoma Christians; a great loss not only for Christianity, but for the history of religion in general.

It seems strange that a form of Christianity should have found such fertile ground in a religious environment so alien to it, but this is where the Thomas school had a great advantage. Unlike other Christianities competing for survival, the St Thomas school seems tailor made for survival in India, since its core doctrines, its method of salvation, and its ascetic sensibilities are nearly identical to those preached by a native Indian religious reformer: the Buddha.

Lost to the West

Meanwhile, in the West, the Thomas Christians declined along with their sister schools of Jewish Christianity. The Gospel of Thomas, however, continued to be valued by various other Christian communities, especially the Gnostics. Since our only complete copy of Thomas comes to us after many centuries of use in Gnostic communities, it is easy to see where Gnostic copyists have embellished it here and there with teachings *en vogue* amongst the Gnostics but which were probably alien to Jewish Christians (such as the verses which imply that the material world and the body are corrupt).

At a council presided over by St Damasus in the fourth century the Pauline Church finally settled on a final list of what books were to be included in the canon of scripture. Until that time, most communities had their own lists of honored books, as well as secondary works which were helpful but not deemed to be inspired. The new list issued by the Council, however, was declared authoritative and superceded local lists. It was also enforced. In the fifth century a new list of "forbidden" books was drawn up, containing those works that the Pauline bishops believed strayed too far from the "accepted" versions. Bishops the world over ordered these works to be destroyed.

Fortunately, there were at least a few monks in Egypt who dissented from this opinion and disobeyed their orders. While they were no doubt sincere monks in the Pauline tradition, they were familiar with these condemned texts and believed that there was information of value in them. Instead of burning them as they had been ordered to do, they put them in a clay jar and carefully sealed the lid to protect them. Then they laid the jar in a cave. When they died, no living soul knew that these forbidden texts still existed, safe and buried in the Egyptian desert. The Gospel of Thomas was one of the books sealed up in that jar.

A Gospel restored to the world

From that time forward, history is silent about the Thomas Gospel until the turn of the 20th century. An archeological dig in the late 1800s in Oxyrhynchus, Egypt, uncovered papyrus fragments containing several sayings attributed to Jesus. They were a startling and intriguing discovery, since they included sayings that had never been heard before. These nineteen "new" sayings were published in 1897 and 1904 and garnered much scholarly interest. Nobody knew that they were part of the Gospel of Thomas until a more complete version of that book was uncovered fifty years later, at Nag Hammadi.

As James M. Robinson tells the story, it was probably in 1945 that a poor Egyptian peasant named Muhammad Ali was digging at the foot of a cliff for soft, rich soil to use as fertilizer. He felt something hard in the dirt, and quickly uncovered a clay jar, tightly sealed at the top. At first he was afraid to open it because he thought it might contain a genie. But then it struck him that it might just as easily contain gold or other riches, and his fear was overcome. He struck the top off of the jar, and fell down in fright at what he thought might be a genie leaping into the air. In fact, says, Robinson, it was probably only dust from the papyrus fragments floating into the air and catching the sunlight.

To Muhammad Ali's extreme disappointment, all he found inside were a bunch of old books. He tore some of the books to divide them between himself and the other camel drivers who were with him, but they didn't want them, either. He placed them in his turban and brought them home, where he dumped them in his family's yard. Over the next few days, his mother used a few of the books as kindling. Then it occurred to him that the books might be worth some money, but he had no luck in selling them, so he traded some of them for cigarettes and fruit. Then an acquaintance noticed that the books were written in Coptic and suggested taking them to a Coptic priest. One volume was indeed passed along to a Coptic priest, who gave it to his brother-in-law, who, in turn, sold it to the Museum in Cairo.

An antique dealer, meanwhile, had caught wind of the find, and sent his agent to investigate. This agent, a man by the name of Bahij Ali, was able to track down many others, some of which he returned to the antique dealer, and some of which he kept to sell himself. Bahij Ali made a good sum on the deal, and bought a luxurious ranch, for which Muhammad Ali's family, who received almost nothing for the find, never forgave him (Robinson, 77-99).

That is not the end of the story, however. Once all of the manuscripts were in the hands of various museums, scholarly and political rivalry kept them in publishing limbo for another thirty years. Fortunately, the Gospel of Thomas was one of the few to see light of day much earlier, as a full English translation was published in 1959. Translated and annotated by British scholar R. Mcl. Wilson, it was released just before Christmas of that year, and the hubbub that resulted sold over forty thousand copies.

A spirituality for today

The Gospel of Thomas, once restored to the world, caused a great deal of interest, both scholarly and popular. Numerous studies were published, followed by defensive dismissals of its contents by conservative Christian scholars. Even now, after nearly fifty years, this amazing work continues to challenge and intrigue Christians and non-Christians alike.

As we shall see in the chapters that follow, Jesus' teachings in this Gospel have a decidedly post-modern ring to them, emphasizing internal over external authority, and promoting a unitive consciousness that is in many ways indistinguishable from the goal held up by many Eastern traditions. In fact, one could argue that the Thomas school is a native Jewish school of Buddhism – a shocking, but completely plausible suggestion.

Far more than any other Gospel available to us today, Thomas presents a Jesus uniquely suited to our contemporary culture. By reading it contemplatively and opening oneself to the shifts in perspective it nudges us to make, it can utterly transform how one sees the world – and oneself.

In the following pages, I offer a new version of the Thomas gospel, designed to be both faithful to the surviving text and easily understandable in contemporary English. It was prepared using Grondin's *Interlinear Coptic/English Translation of the Gospel of Thomas* in comparison with numerous existing English translations, with careful comparison to the Greek fragments found at Oxyrhynchus.

Following the Gospel, we will explore the teachings of the Thomas school in detail, concentrating on the main themes repeatedly emphasized by the text. In addition to describing the teachings as they might have been understood by the early Thomas school, we will also view them in conversation with the mystics of other religious traditions, especially those mystics with whom it shares much in common. Finally, we will mine this Gospel's wisdom for what it can teach us about spirituality for contemporary seekers – the Gospel of Thomas as a relevant and profound spiritual path.

The Gospel of Thomas:
A new version

Prologue These are the hidden words which the living Jesus spoke, and Didymos Judas Thomas wrote down.

Verse 1 And he said, "Whoever happens upon the meaning of these words will not taste Death."

Verse 2 Jesus said, "Let the one who seeks keep on seeking until he finds, and when he finds, he will be troubled, and if he is troubled, he will become surprised, and will become sovereign over all things."

Verse 3 Jesus said, "If those who lead you say to you, 'Look, the kingdom is in the sky,' then the birds will get there before you do. If they say to you, 'It is in the sea,' the fish will get there first. Instead, the kingdom is inside you – and it is outside of you. When you come to know yourselves, then you will be known, and you will realize that you are the children of the living Father. If, however, you do not come to know yourselves, then you dwell in poverty, and you are that poverty.

Verse 4   Jesus said, "A person of great age will not hesitate to ask a little child seven days old about the place of Life, and he will live, for all those who are first will become last, and they will become a single one."

Verse 5   Jesus said, "Know what is before your face, and that which is hidden will be revealed to you. For there is nothing hidden which will not be revealed."

Verse 6   His disciples questioned him, saying, "Do you want us to fast? And how should we pray? Should we give alms? And what foods should we abstain from?" Jesus said, "Do not tell lies, and do not do what you hate, for all things are disclosed to heaven. For there is nothing hidden which will not be revealed, and there is nothing covered that will not be uncovered."

Verse 7   Jesus said, "Blessed is the lion that is eaten by a human, for that lion will become human. And cursed is the human who is eaten by a lion – but the lion will [still] become human."

Verse 8   And he said, "Humans are like a wise fisherman who cast his net into the sea and drew it up from the sea full of little fish from the depths. Among them he found a fine, large fish. So, being a wise fisherman, he cast the little fish back into the water, and easily chose the large fish. He who has ears to hear should listen!

Verse 9   Jesus said, "See here, a sower went out, and, filling his hand with seed, he scattered it. Some fell on the road, and the birds came and snatched it up. Some fell on rock, and so could not send roots down into the earth, and thus no ears rose to the sky. Some fell onto thorns, which choked the seed, and the worms ate them. Some fell on good earth, and good fruit rose to the sky, producing sixty per measure and one hundred twenty per measure.

Verse 10   Jesus said, "I have cast fire upon the world, and see, I am tending it until it burns."

Verse 11   Jesus said, "This heaven will pass away, and the one above it will pass away. And the dead do not live, and the living will not die. In the days when you were eating that which is dead, you were making it alive. When you find yourself in the light, what will you do? On the day you were all one, you made two. When, however, you find yourselves to be two, what will you do then?"

Verse 12   The disciples said to Jesus, "We know that you will leave us. Who will step up, who will lead us?"

Jesus said to them, "Wherever you come from, you should go to James the righteous, for whom heaven and earth came into being."

Verse 13   Jesus said to his disciples, "Compare me with something and tell me what I resemble."

Simon Peter said to him, "You are like a righteous angel."

Matthew said to him, "You are like a wise philosopher."

Thomas said to him, "Master, my mouth is completely incapable of saying what you are like."

Jesus said, "I am not your master, because you have drunk and become intoxicated from the bubbling spring which I have measured out." And he took him and withdrew, and told him three things.

When Thomas, however, returned to his companions, they asked him, "What did Jesus say to you?"

He told them, "If I said to you even one of the things he told me, you would all take up stones and throw them at me, and fire will come out of those stones and burn you all."

Verse 14   Jesus said to them, "If you fast, you will bring forth sin, and if you pray, others will condemn you, and if you give alms, you will create evil in your souls. And if you go into any land, and walk the territories, eat whatever people put in front of you. Heal the sick among them, for it is not what goes into your mouth that will defile you. Rather, it is what comes out of your mouth that will defile you."

Verse 15   Jesus said, "When you look upon the one who is not born of a woman, throw yourself on your face and worship him – for he is your Father."

Verse 16   Jesus said, "Perhaps people are thinking that I have come to cast peace upon the world. What they do not know is that I have come to cast division upon the earth – fire, sword, war. For there will be five people in a house, and three of them will be against the other two, and two against the three; the father will be against the son, and the son against the father; and they will stand to their feet, alone."

Verse 17   Jesus said, "I will give to you what eyes have never seen, what no ear has heard, what hands have not touched, and what has never arisen in the human heart."

Verse 18   The disciples said to Jesus, "Speak to us about our end – in what way will it come?" Jesus said, "Have you uncovered the beginning, so that now you must seek the end? For in the place where the beginning is, the end will be also. Blessed is the one who stands in the beginning; that one will know the end and will not taste death."

Verse 19   Jesus said, "Blessed is the one who was in the beginning, before he came into being. If you want to be my disciples, and listen to my words, even these stones will serve you. For there are five trees in paradise which are undisturbed in summer or winter – their leaves do not even fall. Whoever will know them will not taste death."

Verse 20   The disciples said to Jesus, "Tell us what the kingdom of heaven is like." He told them, "It is like a grain of mustard – the smallest of all the seeds. When, however, it falls to the earth and is given care, it sends out great branches to be shade for the birds of the sky."

Verse 21   Mary said to Jesus, "What do your disciples resemble?"
He answered her, "They resemble small children dwelling in a field which does not belong to them. When the owners of the field come, they will say, 'Give our field back to us.' They will strip naked before them, in order to give everything back, and to return their field. Therefore I say, If the head of the household knows that the burglar is coming, he will keep watch beforehand and will not allow him to sneak into his house – his kingdom! – to steal his possessions. You, however, should all keep watch from the beginning of the world, bind to yourselves great power, so that no thieves will fall upon you on the road, because the help which you look for will fall upon you.
"Let there be in your midst a person who understands. When the fruit split open, he came in a hurry, his sickle in his hand, and he reaped. The one who has ears to hear should listen!"

Verse 22   Jesus watched some babies being nursed. He said to his disciples, "These little ones who are being suckled are like those who go into the Kingdom."

They said to him, "So will we get into the Kingdom by being little ones?"

Jesus said to them, "When you make the two into one, and the inside like the outside, and the outside like the inside, and the top like the bottom, and when you make the male and the female into a single one, so that the male is not male and the female is not female, when you make an eye in the place of an eye and a hand in the place of a hand, and a foot in the place of a foot, and an image in the place of an image, then you will enter the Kingdom."

Verse 23   Jesus said, "I will choose you, one out of a thousand and two out of ten thousand, and they will stand to their feet as one."

Verse 24   His disciples said, "Show us to the place where you are, as it is necessary for us to seek it."

He said to them, "The one who has ears should listen! There is light existing in the inner person of light, which gives light to the whole world; anyone who does not become light is darkness."

Verse 25   Jesus said, "Love your brother like your own soul. Guard him like the pupil of your eye."

Verse 26   Jesus said, "You see the speck in your brother's eye, but you do not see the log in your own eye. When you remove the log from your own eye, then you will be able to see well enough to remove the speck from your brother's eye."

Verse 27   Jesus said, "If you do not fast from the world, you will not find the kingdom. If you do not make the sabbath a sabbath, you will not look upon the Father."

Verse 28 Jesus said, "I stood to my feet in the midst of the world, and outwardly I appeared to them in the flesh. When I came upon them, they were all drunk, and I did not find any of them thirsty. And my soul grieved for the children of humanity, for their minds are blind, and they do not see. For they have come into the world empty, and they seek to leave it empty. But now they are drunk; when they sober up, they will have a change of heart."

Verse 29 Jesus said, "If the flesh came into being because of the spirit, it is a wonder. If spirit came into being because of the body, however, it is a wonder of wonders. Instead, I am amazed at this: how such great richness has come to dwell in such poverty."

Verse 30 Jesus said, "The place which has three gods, all is in god; in the place where there are one or two gods, I am there in it."

Verse 31 Jesus said, "No prophet is accepted in his own village; no physician heals those who know him."

Verse 32 Jesus said, "A city which is being built high upon a mountain, and fortified, will in no way fall, nor can it be hidden."

Verse 33 Jesus said, "What you hear in one ear and the other ear, preach that from the rooftops; for no one burns a lamp and puts it under a leaf, nor does he hide it. Rather he puts it upon a lampstand so that whoever goes in or out may look at its light."

Verse 34   Jesus said, "If a blind person leads a blind person, they both fall into a ditch."

Verse 35   Jesus said, "There is no way a person can enter into the house of a strong man and take him by force, unless he first ties [the strong man's] hands. Then he can loot the house."

Verse 36   Jesus said, "Do not worry from morning to night, or from night until morning about what you will wear."

Verse 37   His disciples said, "When will you be unveiled to us, and when will we look upon you?"

Jesus said, "When you strip yourselves naked without being ashamed, and take your garments and put them under your feet and trample them like little children, then you will look upon the child of the One Who Lives, and you will become fearless."

Verse 38   Jesus said, "Many times you wished to hear the words I am saying to you, and you have no one else to hear them from. But there will come days when you will look for me, and you will not find me."

Verse 39   Jesus said, "The Pharisees and the scribes took the keys of Knowledge and hid them; they neither entered nor allowed anyone who wanted to go in to enter. You, however, be cunning as serpents, and innocent as doves."

Verse 40   Jesus said, "A grapevine has been planted outside the Father, and, cut off from its nourishment, it will be pulled up by its root and destroyed."

Verse 41   Jesus said, "Whoever holds something will be given more, and whoever has little will have even the small amount he possesses taken away."

Verse 42   Jesus said, "Be passers-by."

Verse 43   His disciples said to him, "Who do you think you are, saying such things to us?" He answered, "You do not realize who I am from the things I say. Rather you are like those Jews who either love the tree and hate its fruit, or love the fruit and hate the tree."

Verse 44   Jesus said, "Whoever disrespects the father will be forgiven, and whoever disrespects the son will be forgiven, but whoever disrespects the holy spirit will not be forgiven, neither on earth nor in heaven."

Verse 45   Jesus said, "They do not harvest grapes from thorns, nor do they gather figs out of thistles; for these bear no fruit. A good person brings good things out of his treasure; an evil person brings evil things out of his wicked treasure, his heart, and he speaks evil things. His heart overflows with wicked things."

Verse 46   Jesus said, "From Adam up to John the Baptist, there has been none among those begotten of women greater than John the Baptist, none who should not lower their eyes [in his presence]. But I say that whoever among you will become a little child, you will know the kingdom, and will be greater than John."

Verse 47   Jesus said, "No one can mount two horses at the same time, nor stretch two bows. And there is no way a servant can serve two masters, for he will honor the one, and will despise the other one. No one drinks old wine and immediately desires to drink new wine. And no one pours new wine into old wineskins lest they split open. And they do not pour old wine into new wineskins lest it be ruined. No one sews old patches onto new garments, or they will tear."

Verse 48   Jesus said, "If two people can make peace with one another in one house, they will say to the mountain, 'Move away,' and it will move."

Verse 49   Jesus said, "Blessed are those who are solitary and chosen, for you will find the Kingdom. For you come from it, and you will return to it again."

Verse 50   Jesus said, "If they say to you 'Where do you come from?' Say to them, 'We have come out of the light, the place where the light came of its own accord, and stood to its feet, and appeared to them in their own image.' If they say to you 'Is it you?' say, 'We are its children, and we are the chosen of the living Father.' If they ask you, 'What is the sign of your father within you?' say to them, 'It is movement, and rest.'"

Verse 51   His disciples said to him, "When will the dead find their rest? And when will the new world arrive?" He answered them, "That day you look for has already come. But you, you do not recognize it."

Verse 52   His disciples said to him, "Twenty four prophets spoke in Israel, and they all spoke of you." He said to them, "You have neglected the one who lives in your presence, and speak only of the dead."

Verse 53   His disciples said to him, "Is circumcision a good thing or isn't it?"
   He answered them, "If it were a good thing, fathers would beget sons from their mothers already circumcised. The true circumcision of the spirit, however, is utterly profitable."

Verse 54   Jesus said, "Blessed are the poor, for yours is the Kingdom of Heaven."

Verse 55   Jesus said, "Whoever does not hate his father and mother cannot become my disciple. Whoever does not hate his brothers and sisters, and does not take up his cross as I do is not worthy of me."

Verse 56   Jesus said, "Whoever has come to know the world has discovered a corpse, and whoever has found a corpse, the world is not worthy of him."

Verse 57   Jesus said, "The kingdom of the father is like a man who had good seed. In the night his enemy came and mixed weeds among the good seed. The man did not let them pull up the weeds. He told them, 'Don't pull up the weeds or you might pull up the grain with it. When harvest comes, the weeds will be plain, and they can be pulled up and burned.'"

Verse 58   Jesus said, "Blessed is the one who is troubled and has discovered Life."

Verse 59   Jesus said, "Look to the living one while you are living, lest you die and then seek to see him, and find that you cannot."

Verse 60   A Samaritan was taking a lamb into Judaea. He asked his disciples, "[Why is he carrying] that lamb around [his shoulders]?" They answered, "So that he might kill it and eat it." He said to them, "He will not eat it while it is alive; rather if he kills it, it becomes a corpse." They said, "He cannot do it, otherwise." He said to them, "You yourselves should seek after a place of peace so that you will not become corpses and be eaten yourselves."

Verse 61   Jesus said, "Two people will rest upon a bed; one will die, and one will live."

Salome said, "Who are you, man? You have climbed

onto my bed and eaten from my table as if you were someone [important]."

Jesus said to her, "I am one who comes from where all is equal; they gave me that which is of my Father."

"I am your disciple."

"Because of this, I say that when he is destroyed, he will be full of light. But when he is divided, he will be full of darkness."

Verse 62   Jesus said, "I speak my mysteries to those who are worthy of them. Do not let your left hand know what your right hand is doing."

Verse 63   Jesus said, "There was a man of great wealth who possessed many riches. He said, 'I will make use of my riches, so that I might sow and reap and plant and fill my storehouse with fruit, so that I will never lack for anything.' These were the thoughts he entertained about his riches, and yet that same night, he died. He who has ears should listen!"

Verse 64   Jesus said, "A man was hosting some visitors, and when he had prepared a feast he sent his servant to call the visitors. He went to the first and said to him, 'My lord calls for you.' He answered, 'I have some money intended for some merchants; they are meeting me tonight, and I must go and place my order. I beg to be excused from the dinner.'

"So he went to another of the visitors. He said to him, 'My lord has called for you.' He answered him, 'I have bought a house, and am required all day – no rest for me!'

"So he went to another one, and said to him, 'My lord calls you.' He answered him, 'My friend is getting married, and I have to prepare the dinner. I can't come, and ask to be excused from the feast.'

"He went to another, and said to him, 'My lord calls for you.' But he said, 'I have bought a farm, and must go collect the rent. I can't come, and hope to be excused.'

"The servant went back to his lord and said, 'All those you invited to your feast have begged off.'

"The lord said to his servant, 'Go outside, to the streets, and whomever you meet, bring them in to dine.'

"The buyers and the traders may not enter the places of my Father."

Verse 65 He said, "A just man had a vineyard, which he entrusted to some tenants that they might work in it, and yield for him its fruit. He sent his servant to collect grapes from the tenants of the vineyard. They grabbed his servant and beat him, and nearly killed him. The servant went and reported to his lord. His lord said, 'Perhaps they did not recognize him.' So he sent another servant. The tenants beat the other servant. Then the lord sent his son, saying, 'Perhaps they will be ashamed before my son.' Because the tenants recognized the heir to the vineyard, they seized him and killed him. He who has ears should listen!"

Verse 66 Jesus said, "Show me the stone that the builders rejected; that is the cornerstone."

Verse 67 Jesus said, "Whoever knows the All, but needs himself, needs everything."

Verse 68 Jesus said, "Blessed are you who are hated and persecuted, for no place will be found where you have been persecuted."

Verse 69   Jesus said, "Blessed are those who have been persecuted in their hearts, for there they have known the Father in truth. Blessed are those who are hungry, so they may satisfy the bellies of those who desire."

Verse 70   Jesus said, "When you bring forth that which is within you, that which you bring forth will save you. If you do not bring forth what is within you, what you fail to bring forth will destroy you."

Verse 71   Jesus said, "I will destroy this house, and no one will ever build it again."

Verse 72   A man said to him, "Speak to my brothers so that they may divide my father's belongings with me."

He answered him, "Mister, who made me a divider?"

He turned to his disciples, and said, "Honestly, am I a divider?"

Verse 73   Jesus said, "The harvest is plentiful indeed; the laborers, however, are few. Pray, therefore, to the Lord so that he might send laborers out to the harvest."

Verse 74   He said, "Lord, there are many around the water fountain, but nothing in the well."

Verse 75   Jesus said, "There are many standing at the door, but the solitaries are the ones who will go into the bridal chamber."

Verse 76   Jesus said, "The Father's Kingdom can be compared to a merchant who had some stock and found a pearl. The merchant was wise – he returned his stock and bought the pearl for himself alone. Even so, you should seek after the treasure which endures and does not perish, where no moth can eat it nor worms destroy it."

Verse 77   Jesus said, "I am the light which is above all things. I am the All, from me all things have emerged and to me all things have been revealed. Split the wood, and I am there; lift the stone, and you will find me there."

Verse 78   Jesus said, "Why did you come out to the fields? To see a reed waving about in the wind? And to see a man wearing soft garments like your kings and those in power? They are clad in soft garments and cannot know the truth."

Verse 79   A woman in the crowd said to him, "Blessed is she whose belly bore you and whose breasts nourished you."

   Jesus said to her, "Blessed are they who have listened to the word of the father; truly they have been mindful of him! For days are coming when you will say, 'Blessed is she whose bellies did not conceive, and whose breasts gave no milk.'"

Verse 80   Jesus said, "Whoever has known the world has found a body. But the world is not worthy of the one who has found the body."

Verse 81   Jesus said, "Whoever has become rich should become king, and the one who has power should renounce it."

Verse 82   Jesus said, "Whoever is near me is near the fire, and whoever is far from me is far from the Kingdom."

Verse 83   Jesus said, "Images are revealed to people, and the light within them is hidden in the image of the light of the father. He will be revealed and his image hidden by his light."

Verse 84   Jesus said, "In the days when you look upon your likeness, you rejoice. When, however, you look upon your images as they were in the beginning, which are eternal and yet have never become manifest, how much will you be able to bear?"

Verse 85   Jesus said, "Adam came to be out of a great power and great wealth, and yet he did not become worthy of you. For if he was worthy he would not have tasted death."

Verse 86   Jesus said, "Foxes have their holes and birds have their nests, there. A human being, however, does not have a place to lay her head and rest."

Verse 87   Jesus said, "Wretched is the body that depends on a body, and wretched is the soul that depends on these two."

Verse 88   Jesus said, "The angels are coming to you, along with the prophets, and they will give you what is yours. And you, also, will give them what you have, and will say to yourselves, 'When will they come to take what is theirs?'"

Verse 89   Jesus said, "For what reason do you wash the outside of a cup? Don't you understand that whoever created the inside is the same one who made the outside?"

Verse 90   Jesus said, "Come to me, for my yoke is easy, and my lordship is gentle, and you will find rest."

Verse 91   They said to him, "Tell us who you are, so that we may believe in you." He said to them, "You read the face of the heavens and the earth, and yet you did not recognize the one who was in your presence; and you do not know how to read the present moment."

Verse 92   Jesus said, "Seek, and you will find. Yet those things you used to ask me about, I did not answer you then. But now it pleases me to speak of them, and you have stopped seeking."

Verse 93   Jesus said, "Do not give holy things to the dogs, so that they will not cast them unto the dung-heap. Do not cast the pearls to swine, so that they… *(rest of verse missing in original manuscript)*

Verse 94   Jesus said, "He who seeks will find, and the doors will be opened for him who is called in."

Verse 95   Jesus said, "If you have money, do not lend it with interest. Instead, give it to someone who can give you nothing back."

Verse 96   Jesus said, "The kingdom of the father is like a woman who took a little bit of leaven, hid it within some dough, and made it into huge loaves of bread. He who has ears should listen!"

Verse 97   Jesus said, "The kingdom of the father is like a woman carrying a jar full of meal. While she was walking on a road far away, the handle of the jar broke, and the meal emptied out after her upon the road. She didn't notice that anything was wrong, and when she entered her house she put the jar down and discovered it was empty."

Verse 98   Jesus said, "The kingdom of the father is like a man who wanted to kill a powerful man. In his house, he drew a sword, and stuck it into the wall so that he might know whether he had the skill to do it. Then he killed the powerful man."

Verse 99   The disciples said to him, "Your brothers and your mother are standing outside."

He said to them, "Those here who do the will of my Father, these are my brothers and my mother; it is they who will go into the Kingdom of my father."

Verse 100   They showed Jesus a coin, and said to him, "Caesar's people are demanding taxes of us." He said to them, "Give to Caesar what belongs to Caesar, give to God what belongs to God, and give to me what belongs to me."

Verse 101   He said to them, "Whoever does not hate their father and mother, as I do, cannot become my disciple. And whoever does not love their father and mother, as I do, cannot become my disciple. For my mother...gave birth to my body, but my true mother gave me life."

Verse 102   Jesus said, "Woe to the Pharisees, for they are like a dog resting on the oxen's manger – it neither eats, nor allows the oxen to eat."

Verse 103   Jesus said, "Blessed is the man who knows where the thieves will enter, so that he may get up and gather his community, and be prepared before they come in."

Verse 104   They said to Jesus, "Come, pray and fast today."

Jesus replied, "What sin have I committed? How have I been defeated? Instead, when the bridegroom leaves the bridal chamber, then let them fast and pray."

Verse 105   Jesus said, "Whoever comes to know the father and the mother will be referred to as 'the son of a whore.'"

Verse 106   Jesus said, "When you make the two into one, you will become the Sons of Man, and if you should say, 'Mountain, move away!' it will move."

Verse 107   Jesus said, "The kingdom is like a shepherd who had a hundred sheep. The largest of these went astray. The shepherd left the other ninety-nine and looked for the one until he found it. He was very worried, and told the sheep, 'I love you more than the ninety-nine.'"

Verse 108   Jesus said, "Whoever drinks out of my mouth, he will become like me; I also will be as he is, and that which is hidden will be revealed to him."

Verse 109   Jesus said, "The kingdom is like a man who had a treasure hidden in his field that he did not know about. And after his death, he left it to his son. The son also did not know [about it]. He took over the field and sold it. The person who bought it went plowing, and he found the treasure, and began to lend the money at interest to whomever he pleased."

Verse 110   Jesus said, "Whoever has found the world and become rich, let him renounce the world."

Verse 111   Jesus said, "The heavens, along with the earth, will be rolled up in your presence; and he who lives out of the one who lives will not look upon death." After all, Jesus says whoever finds himself, of him the world is not worthy.

Verse 112   Jesus said, "Woe to the flesh that depends on the soul, and woe to the soul that depends on the flesh."

Verse 113   His disciples asked him, "When will the Kingdom arrive?" [Jesus answered,] "It is not coming in a way you can see outwardly. No one is going to say, 'Look, over there!' or 'There it is!' Rather, the Kingdom of the Father is spread out upon the earth, and people do not see it."

Verse 114   Simon Peter said, "Let Mary depart from us, for women are not worthy of Life."

Jesus answered, "Behold, I will lead her, and I will make her male so that she might also be a living spirit like you males. For any woman who makes herself male, she will enter the Kingdom of heaven...."

THE
NINE INSIGHTS

There is only one thing in the universe, and you are that thing

The day of my spiritual awakening was the day I saw,
and knew I saw, all things in God, and God in all things.
— Mechtild of Magdeburg (42)

As you've gathered by now, the verses of the Thomas Gospel can be maddeningly obscure. I would be surprised if you read very far without saying, "What in the world...??" with a furrowed, puzzled brow. Worry not, this is entirely by design. The verses are *supposed* to be obscure and confusing. Thomas (and perhaps the Jesus of Thomas) is employing an ancient device designed to draw you deeper into the text, beyond the surface meaning. Like the koan in the Zen tradition, the intent is to initially confound the student, with the hope that, given sufficient rumination, the true meaning will suddenly occur, a flash of insight that not only makes sense of the verses, but also brings with it *satori*, enlightenment, or in Christian terminology, salvation.

If this is what you are after, read no further. It will do you no good if someone simply *tells* you what it means. For the Gospel to be truly salvific, you will have to work it the way the ancient Thomas Christians (and Zen Buddhists through the ages) have done it – the hard way. Stop reading, turn back to the beginning of the translation, and meditate. It might take you years, but if you want to be enlightened, this is the way to do it. Unfortunately, few of us can devote the time and effort it takes to become truly enlightened. This book is written for "the rest of us," who can't leave everything behind to go meditate in the desert, but still hope to find some spiritual guidance.

There is an interpretive key that makes sense of all the weird and confusing symbology in this Gospel. Once you have that key, everything will fall into place, and you will be able to read through the Gospel, if not with total clarity, at least with a much greater level of comprehension.

This key is unspoken in the Gospel. It is alluded to, spoken of obliquely, but never directly expressed. Nonetheless, once the key has been spoken, interpreting Thomas is much easier. It may be that Jesus gave this key orally. He certainly would have given it secretly, and there is no way it ever could have been written down in his own time, because it would have been considered heretical. In fact, Jesus may not have been so successful in keeping this teaching a secret, as he was killed for heresy, although the Pauline gospels understand this in quite a different way.

The key is this: There is only one thing in the universe, *and you are that thing.* Call it God, call it Unity, call it what you will. All names fall short (although the Hebrew name for God, YWHW, which translates, "I am what I am becoming," is not a bad one). All distinctions are illusory, and suffering and sin are visited upon us as a result of our buying into this illusion. All is One, and *you are that One.*

This is nothing new, of course, to students of mysticism of any variety. Thomas falls squarely into the same camp as other unitive schools of thought such as Taoism, Hinduism, and Buddhism. Thomas' Jesus is trying to prod us into a state of unitive consciousness, in which we realize: the unity of God with all things (including us human beings), unity within the self, and our mystical unity with one another. All of these are aspects of a single phenomenon of Oneness, simply viewed from different perspectives: from the outside looking in, from the inside looking out, and the horizontal view, as illusory aspects of reality relate to one another. The Gospel of Thomas focuses on each of these perspectives, and in the process, relates a sublime truth that is at once slippery and simple.

Unity of God with all things

If we accept the idea that there is only one thing in the universe, and we agree to call that thing God, then it stands to reason that all things that appear to have separate existence are part of that one thing, and participate in its unity. This teaching can have a profound effect on us, because, of course, that means that we, too, are part of that one thing.

I remember several years ago I was lying out under the stars, filled with wonder at the vastness of the universe. I had a moment of vertigo as I realized that the universe was singular, that it was one thing, and that it included me (I was glad I was laying down when the realization struck). "The universe is me, too." I breathed aloud, and wondered deeply at this revelation. *I am the universe.* I hadn't yet connected this realization to God, but it was not a huge leap, and that further revelation was not long in coming. But I trace the genesis of my personal mystical awakening to that moment, as the seeds of all subsequent epiphanies have their beginning there, on that California hillside.

Nicholas of Cusa, a medieval Christian mystic, explores this realization further, when he writes, "In every creature the universe is the creature; consequently, each creature receives the whole, so that in any creature all creatures are found, in a relative way. The universe is in each person in such a way that each person is in it, and so every person in the universe *is* the universe" (52).

Jesus was no stranger to this experience, for as I have said, this realization is the key to all of his teaching in the Thomas Gospel. In verse 77, he says, "I am the light which is above all things. I am the All, from me all things have emerged and to me all things have been revealed. Split the wood, and I am there; lift the stone, and you will find me there."

In the first part of this verse, Jesus speaks not as a rabbi, an earthbound human being, but from the perspective of the entirety. Because he has been enlightened, because he has experienced unitive consciousness, "all things have been revealed" to him, and he can therefore speak from this perspective: "I am the All, from me all things have emerged."

It is because of his identity with the One that he can utter what are some of the most beautiful and mystical words in this Gospel: "Split the wood, and I am there; lift the stone, and you will find me there." Of course, he does not mean that if you split a log, you will find a little rabbi inside. He means that just as this log is part of the One, you can find the One hidden in the depths of even the most mundane of objects, even a log.

Another Christian mystic, Hildegard of Bingen, speaks from a similar cosmic perspective when she writes, "I am the one whose praise echoes on high. I adorn all the earth. I am the breeze that nurtures all things green. I encourage blossoms to flourish with ripening fruits. I am led by the Spirit to feed the purest streams. I am the rain coming from the dew that causes the grasses to laugh with the joy of life. I call forth tears, the aroma of holy work. I am the yearning for good" (31).

Whether this is pantheism (the idea that the universe and God are synonymous) or pan*en*theism (the idea that the universe is within God, but that God is more than the phenomenal universe) I will leave up to you, the reader, to decide for yourself. The Thomas Gospel takes no position on this. And it may be that such distinctions are, once again, simply part of the illusion and, ultimately, academic. The experience of Oneness is what is important to Thomas' Jesus, not speculations about the limits of that Oneness.

Like many mystical schools, the point in the Thomas Gospel is to see through the illusion of separateness – all separateness, at any level – to behold the essential unity of being. As the Zen poet writes in the *Blue Cliff Record*:

> Within myriad forms, only one body is revealed;
> > Only when one is sure for himself will he then be near.
> > In past years I mistakenly turned to the road to search;
> > Now I look upon it like ice within fire (43).

As this poem suggests, this is not information that can simply be related. It must be experienced, for one can only be "near" enlightenment when one knows this unity for oneself. The answer is not found by searching, by wandering the many roads in a quest for enlightenment, for the answer is not found "out there." Like "ice within fire" the answer is paradoxical. The verse suggests that this awareness is vulnerable, even ephemeral, as ice does not last long in contact with heat. But it also suggests that knowledge of the infinite is to be found within.

Internal unity of oneself

Oneness is not only about my union with the universe, those things I perceive to be outside of myself, but also about the union of all of my internal parts. If it is true that "charity begins at home," then it is no less true that oneness begins there, too. In verse 22, Jesus is watching some babies being nursed. He said to his disciples, "These little ones who are being suckled are like those who go into the Kingdom."

They said to him, "So will we get into the Kingdom by being little ones?"

Jesus said, "When you make the two into one, and the inside like the outside, and the outside like the inside, and the top like the bottom, and when you make the male and the female into a single one, so that the male is not male and the female is not female, when you make an eye in the place of an eye and a hand in the place of a hand, and a foot in the place of a foot, and an image in the place of an image, then you will enter the Kingdom."

This is a profound teaching, and bears much consideration. Jesus is telling the disciples how to enter the Kingdom (we'll discuss the Kingdom at length in a later chapter – for now, it is enough for us to imagine it to be the state of unitive consciousness we are seeking), and suggests that one must be like a child to do it. This puzzles the disciples, but Jesus' explanation seems even more confounding. The first thing he says they must do is to "make the two into one." This is a statement of his basic teaching on Unity, the elimination of all dualisms. When you perceive any two (or more) things as only One thing, then you know you have "made it." But as long as we perceive an "us" and a "them," a "me" and a "you," or an "heaven" and an "earth," then clearly, we have not yet penetrated the core of this teaching. The experience of unitive consciousness collapses all "two-ness" into the One.

The next admonition is to make "the inside like the outside, and the outside like the inside." Not only must we eliminate the illusion of distinction between ourselves and the outer universe, but we must eliminate internal dualisms as well. We all have various "personas," different faces we show to others in different contexts, and each of these "faces" is different than the person we perceive ourselves to be, inside. These are all mechanisms that we learn for survival, but like many coping mechanisms that helped us in childhood, as adults such devices rarely serve us and must be reexamined.

In order to reach a state of unity, all "false faces" must be discarded, along with all pretensions. We must simply be who we are. This is not an easy task, for often we have not been honest even with ourselves about who we really are. We have been socialized to lie so much that it is impossible to live without lying, even to ourselves.

Internal unity means being honest to the degree that we are willing to let go of the lies we tell each other and ourselves, achieving an inner-outer congruity that makes interior dualism possible. We must be the same person inside and out, or we will continue wasting our energy on hiding, even though we are often not even conscious that we have been doing it. Such is Julian of Norwich's prayer, when she expresses her hope that, "with his grace [the Lord] has led and evermore shall join the Outer Face with the Inner Face and makes us all one with him and each of us one with another in true lasting joy that is Jesus" (116). Congruity between our inner and outer selves is a very difficult task, and a fit project for the therapist's couch. It is certainly not an aspect that anyone on a serious spiritual path should neglect.

One way we have been lied to, and continue to lie to ourselves, regards the distinction between masculine and feminine. The next part of this verse, "when you make the male and the female into a single one, so that the male is not male and the female is not female," speaks directly to this issue. No human being is *only* female or *only* male. We all contain masculine and feminine qualities, and personal integrity demands that both qualities be acknowledged, nurtured, and expressed.

We are far more fortunate than those in ages past in this regard, as gender roles are less rigid than ever before. The feminist movement of the early 1970s gave women permission to give expression to such masculine qualities as leadership, independence, and ambition. Though we still have a ways to go in terms of full equality for women in our society, great progress has been made. Even though there are still some resentful holdouts for traditional gender roles (such as the recent Vatican pronouncement on the proper place of women in society), the battle is over and even young women who don't style themselves as "feminists" take for granted much that the feminist movement fought so hard for.

Men had their turn in the 1980s, as the various men's movements made it okay – even hip – to cry, nurture others, and recite poetry while drumming naked in the woods. Great progress indeed! As a card-carrying SNAG (sensitive new-age guy), I can attest that it is much easier to be me now than it was when I was a child. The admonitions to "suck it up and take it like a man" didn't sit well with this child (does it for any?) and the societal pressure to quell my emotions and present a tough-guy exterior at all times was profoundly oppressive. Now, I feel comfortable weeping openly at the movies and asking for directions when lost. It is truly a different world.

It has been a great boon for both men and women to be permitted by society – and even encouraged – to integrate both their masculine and feminine natures. I dare say it has been a boon for society in general, and certainly for coming generations of girls and boys, who presumably will not be told that they may not (respectively) be president or homemakers if they want to.

This teaching of inner integration may have its roots in an ancient tradition of Jewish mysticism, since it pops up not only in Thomas, but also in later Jewish mystical writings as well. The medieval mystical text the *Zohar* states that, "Blessings are found only where male and female are found, as is written: 'He blessed them and called their name Adam on the day they were created.' It is not written: 'He blessed him and called his name Adam.' A human being is only called Adam when male and female are as one" (23).

We are only truly human when we men can embrace our inner female, and women likewise find their humanity when they can integrate their inner male. This truth is stated again by Thomas' Jesus in a controversial passage. Verse 114 states, "Simon Peter said, 'Let Mary depart from us, for women are not worthy of Life.' Jesus answered, 'Behold, I will lead her, and I will make her male so that she might also be a living spirit like you males. For any woman who makes herself male, she will enter the Kingdom of Heaven.'"

This has widely been interpreted as an extremely sexist verse. But I believe the original version went on to read: "...And any man who makes himself female, will likewise enter the Kingdom." This is certainly congruent with Jesus' other teachings in this book, and it is all too easy to see how a celibate male scribe in the third century would have felt threatened by the second half of the verse, and conveniently just neglected to transcribe it when copying the text.

This teaching is found in ancient pagan sources, as well. In Plato's *Symposium*, there is recounted a myth of how the sexes came into being. Originally, we were all androgynous, being both male and female, living in Edenic bliss. But, like Prometheus or the builders of Babel, we lusted after those things that belong to the gods alone. As punishment, we were hewn in two, becoming male and female. The belly button is the remaining scar of our separation. We are warned to honor the gods properly in the future or we will once again be hewn in two, which would leave us all hopping around on one leg. Our goal in this myth is to seek out our lost half so that we may return to a state of bliss.

While this myth has largely been interpreted as meaning we must find our opposite-sex soul mate in order to achieve oneness, it is not hard to imagine that an inner joining of these two halves might also be suggested by the myth, and may indeed be our true work.

Another tradition in which this joining has been mythically externalized is in Gnosticism. According to some sects of early Christian Gnostics, the separation of Christ from his consort, Sophia, is partly responsible for the existence of the phenomenal universe, which in Gnostic teaching, is not a good place to be. The universe for the Gnostics is chaotic, corrupt, and horribly flawed, if not downright evil.

One of the Valentinian Gnostic sacraments is the Bridal Chamber. In this ritual, the man assumes the identity of Christ, while the woman assumes the identity of Sophia. In their sexual union, the dualism of the universe is symbolically healed, and the power of the evil spiritual forces which govern the world is broken, leaving the participants in the ritual free to escape the bonds of the phenomenal universe, and to finally join the Oneness, or the "Fullness" as they called it, after their deaths.

In the Thomas Gospel, this union of male and female is an entirely interior process, and one which all of us must undergo in order to heal the wound of dualism inflicted upon us by society. It is a learning, and an unlearning. Rilke wrote, "We contain multitudes." The goal of the mystic is to embrace, integrate, and embody all of them.

Unity of inside with outside

But Jesus is asking us to go even further. We are invited to not only neutralize internal dualities, but even the distinction between internal and external. In Zen teaching, the idea that we are separate creatures is an illusion, and the ego that we have built up for ourselves, this "I" with which we refer to ourselves, is also an illusion. Thomas Merton, a Twentieth-century Christian mystic, says that "when the...identity of the ego is taken to be my deepest and only identity, when I am thought to be nothing but the sum total of all my relationships, when I cling to this self and make it the center around which and for which I live, I then make my empirical identity into the False Self. My own self then becomes the obstacle to realizing my true self" (Finley, p. 18).

Transpersonal psychology has done much to explain this phenomenon. According to transpersonal theorist Michael Washburn, when we are first born we are not conscious of any distinction between ourself and our mother, between ourself and the outside world. The Dynamic Ground of All Being (the greater Self of which we are all a part) and our consciousness are one, and archetypal energies from the collective unconscious wash over us constantly. But we cannot survive being assaulted by so much information, and soon we develop an ego. This is a wall built around the Dynamic Ground which blocks out the deluge of archetypal information, and creates a false sense of separateness, an "I" that is conscious of itself as a being separate from the Dynamic Ground, and from other beings.

This "I" serves us well as we grow into adulthood, but eventually we run into trouble. The false sense of distinction drives us to behave in selfish, even evil ways, creating tragedies from poverty to genocide. "Us" vs. "them" is the ego operating on a social scale, and untold horrors have followed in its wake.

Eventually, if we are to answer the call of what is within us, we must recognize the ego-wall we have built for what it is: another façade, a false distinction that once served us well. In clinging to the illusion that this ego is *us*, we perpetuate the suffering that plagues us. We know that something is very wrong, and we scramble to fill the void we instinctively feel inside us in the only way we know how. We have been well trained as consumers, and our addictive rush towards anything that will pacify us, however temporarily, reveals the depths of our individual and cultural bondage. The ego is itself this fragmentation, the very thing that cuts us off from wholeness.

The Zen practitioner realizes that the ego-self is, in Merton's words, "not final or absolute; it is a provisional self-construction which exists, for practical purposes, only in a sphere of relativity.

Its existence has meaning in so far as it does not become fixated or centered upon itself as ultimate" (*Zen ...*, p. 26).

Of course, once we begin to realize some of this, the ego invariably feels threatened (with good reason!) and switches into survival mode, fighting with everything it has for its continued sovereignty, sometimes causing "spiritual emergencies" and psychotic episodes that are really "spiritual *emergences*." Even so, the ego may play along for a while, and allow us our forays into spirituality and meditation, allowing it to be stretched almost to the vanishing point, but so long as it can "snap back" and regain control once the meditation period ends, we are still acting out of the False Self.

"As long as there is an 'I' that is the definite subject of a contemplative experience," writes Merton, "an 'I' that is aware of itself and its contemplation, an 'I' that can possess a certain 'degree of spirituality,' then we have not yet passed over the Red Sea, we have not yet 'gone out of Egypt.' We remain in the realm of multiplicity, activity, incompleteness, striving, and desire" (Finley, 130).

Eventually, if we are to be whole, we must make a crack in the ego-wall, and reestablish a relationship with the Dynamic Ground, and once again allow the archetypal energies to flood over us. This is often scary, even terrifying, but once the ego is revealed to be a fake, and we are once again conscious of our union with the Dynamic Ground (or the universe, or God, or whatever you want to call the Larger Self of which we are a part), then we have returned to the place where we began. Like little children, we perceive no distinction between the Dynamic Ground and ourselves, and we are once again open to the rush of transpersonal information available to us – "all things are revealed" to us, in Jesus words – and we find ourselves, inexplicably, in the Kingdom.

Suzuki says, "If you want to seek the Buddha, you ought to see into your own Nature, which is the Buddha himself. The Buddha is a free man – a man who neither works nor achieves. If, instead...you turn away and seek the Buddha in external things, you will never get at him" (10). The great Ch'an master Hui-neng agrees, saying, "the deluded mind looks outside itself to seek the Buddha, not yet realizing that its own self-nature is Buddha" (11).

Jesus speaks to this process in the Gospel of Thomas, when he says, "Two people will rest upon a bed; one will die, and one will live" (61). The "two people" are really one (big surprise!): your ego, and your True Self. In order for the True Self to really live, to gain eternal life, the ego must die. This verse continues in the form of a conversation between Jesus and a woman named Salome:

Salome said, "Who are you, man? You have climbed onto my bed and eaten from my table as if you were someone [important]."

Jesus said to her, "I am one who comes from where all is equal; they gave me that which is of my father."

"I am your disciple."

"Because of this, I say that when he is destroyed, he will be full of light. But when he is divided, he will be full of darkness."

Only when the ego has been deprived of its relentless illusion of sovereignty – and its power destroyed – will a person be "filled with light," or, as we might say today, enlightened. But note the second half of that verse, for it is a warning: "But when he is divided, he will be full of darkness." All divisions, inner or outer, frustrate our journey towards life. Every illusion of separateness that we cling to impedes our illumination.

Unity with other peoples

Not only does Jesus call us to be conscious of our unity with God, with the world around us, and of our own internal unity, but he also calls us to see ourselves as one with all the other people around us, as well. Jesus' admonition in the canonical Gospel of Matthew, "Whatsoever you do to the least of these my brothers, you do unto me" (25:40) is not to be interpreted symbolically, but literally, as Jesus sees no distinction between himself and the lowly beggar. This kind of attitude is what so horrified his co-religionists as he sat at table with prostitutes and traitors – for he saw no difference between himself and them. They are One.

Jesus speaks of the power inherent in this knowledge, when in verse 48 he says, "If two people can make peace with one another in one house, they will say to the mountain, 'Move away,' and it will move." This is not just a quaint verse about the power of a good marriage, but a reminder that the unity of peoples – even two peoples – brings with it the potential for transformative and cosmic power.

That this verse may in fact be about internal unity is spoken by a similar Buddhist scripture, "A monk who is skilled in concentration can cut the Himalayas in two" (Anguttara Nikaya 6:24). Concentration unites the parts, creates unity, and this creates power. And certainly this is one way to understand this verse. But the social dimensions suggested by this verse are equally applicable, and not to be ignored. Nicholas of Cusa speaks to this interpretation when he writes, "When there is one mind among many, there you find peace and strength. Those of one mind dwell in the divine home" (117).

We come closest to realizing this unity with one another in sexual union, but that is only a small taste of the unity that is already present and operative in us, if only we could see it. Sexuality is sacramental; it is a symbolic foretaste of the union which we may someday fully enjoy. Such sexual schools of enlightenment as Tantra and the Gnostic ritual we discussed earlier are evidence of the great value of such sacramental approaches. The union of my being with this one other (my sexual partner) is metonymous of my union with all other peoples, including Jesus himself.

The medieval mystics were fond of such erotic double entendres. Julian of Norwich wrote, "God wants to be thought of as our Lover. I must see myself so bound in love as if everything that has been done has been done for me. That is to say, the Love of God makes such a unity in us that when we see this unity no one is able to separate oneself from one another" (113).

Jesus speaks of our union with one another in ways that are unabashedly salvific. In verse four, he says, "A person of great age will not hesitate to ask a little child seven days old about the place of Life, and he will live, for all those who are first will become last, and they will become a single one."

This verse turns on its ear the Jewish prophetic tradition which promises that kings and potentates will, in the next world, be reduced to servants, while the poor and oppressed will, in the next life, rule over those who oppressed them. "The mountains will be made low, and every valley shall be exalted," (Is. 40:4) is not speaking about Palestinian topography, but about people and their social stations. Likewise, the Jesus of Thomas suggests that the newborn may in fact be more knowledgeable about the whole than a man wise in years – the child is still in contact with the Dynamic Ground, after all, and has far less to unlearn than the old man. But the old man is truly wise, for he does not hesitate to humble himself and ask the newborn for help. The valley is exalted, and the mountain is indeed brought low. All things are equal (remember that Jesus said that he comes from a place where all things are equal in verse 61), and the realization of unity is not far from us.

Likewise, Jesus tells us in verse 23, "I will choose you, one out of a thousand and two out of ten thousand, and they will stand to their feet as one." Jesus is not imagining that everyone will reach this consciousness. Instead, he suggests that it is a rare realization, reached only by a couple of people out of every ten thousand. Yet, these two will emerge into the world as a single being, united in mind, purpose, and hope of eternal life.

We are not separate beings, fighting tooth and claw for our individual survival. We are one, and much of the suffering of the world might be alleviated if we truly understood that. Similarly, we are not simply one with other human beings, but with all creatures, and indeed with the earth herself. If only we could internalize what Chief Seattle said so succinctly, "Humankind has not woven the web of life. We are but one thread within it. Whatever we do to the web, we do to ourselves. All things are bound together. All things connect."

A call for change

Jesus' teachings of unity can have a profound effect on us. To follow the Way of Thomas is to acknowledge the ways in which our reality has been fragmented; indeed the ways in which we ourselves have been fragmented. Everything in our society is designed to support and perpetuate this fragmentation. From the caste system of ancient

India to the contemporary social stratification that dictates, "who will serve and who will eat" (as Leonard Cohen so poetically put it), human beings have long been socialized to see division where Heaven sees none. Cartographers are most fond of drawing lines that separate countries, counties, and cities, and yet from space no such divisions are visible, nor do the creatures, which share this earth with us, have any use for such arbitrary divisions.

We have much "unlearning" to do if we are to achieve the state of unitive consciousness that Jesus calls us to. Yet seeing the problem is the first step towards the solution. The very recognition of our "two-ness" is a call to change, to reevaluation of ourselves and our place in the universe.

On the surface of it, it may also seem like a call to the irrational and the impractical, perhaps even the impossible. Jesus does not really help by saying such things as, "This heaven will pass away, and the one above it will pass away. And the dead do not live, and the living will not die. In the days when you were eating that which is dead, you were making it alive."

But then he balances such metaphysical obliqueness with passages of startling clarity, as when this verse continues: "When you find yourself in the light, what will you do? On the day you were all one, you made two. When, however, you find yourselves to be two, what will you do then?" (11).

So this is the question before us: Now that you know you have been fragmented, what are you going to do about it? "When you find yourselves to be two, what will you do then?" We have a decision before us, and this requires us to choose, and we should remember that not choosing is also making a choice. We suffer because we think we are separate beings, an illusion of division that reaches even into our own psyches, our souls, separating us from our own true identity.

The Way of Thomas not only confronts us with this question, but provides the means for healing the dualism that plagues us. The Jesus of Thomas calls us to wholeness, not a superficial integration of our divergent longings and impulses, but a wholeness that transcends limits. Jesus calls us to wholeness not only within ourselves, but also in relation to one another and the universe itself. He calls us to spiritual wholeness, by recognizing and living into our unity with God.

But how do we reach the goal of unitive consciousness that Jesus calls us to? Does it come all at once, or in stages? Do we reach it on our own, or do others have a part to play in our awakening? Once we acknowledge the need for the journey, how do we find the road?

Spiritual exercises

1. **Practice embracing all of your parts.** Every time you become aware of a part of yourself – an attitude, a talent, a fault, even a hint of meanness, say to this part, "I embrace you and love you." Say this especially about all the things you really hate about yourself. This will be extremely uncomfortable, but utterly transforming if you can keep up the practice.

2. The Hindus have a saying, "Tat Tvam Asi," which means "Thou art that," or "This is you, too." As you go about your workday, keep this saying on your tongue. **Whomever or whatever you encounter, say to yourself, "You are that,"** before you engage with him, her, or it. Let the truth of your unity with these people, animals, and things you encounter sink in. Trust the truth of it, and practice, so that you encounter each new person or thing with an awareness of your unity with him, her, or it.

When you can see what is right in front of you, the hidden things will be revealed as well

Woman! Your soul has slept from childhood on.
Now, it is awakened by the light of true love.
In this light the soul looks around her to discover
who it is who is showing Himself to her here.
Now, she sees clearly, she recognizes for
the first time how God is all in all.

— Mechtild of Magdeburg (82)

Unfortunately for those of us of a bookish bent, simply knowing that we are all one is not the same as the *experience* of oneness. And it is this experience that is the true knowing. This is the difference between head knowledge and heart knowledge: anyone can parrot facts (or even ancient wisdom), but actually internalizing and living out of such wisdom is another matter altogether, and it is this true knowing that the Jesus of Thomas desires for us.

Meister Eckhart knew this distinction well. He tells us, "Whatever I want to express in its truest meaning must emerge from within me and pass through an inner form. It cannot come from outside to the inside but must emerge from within" (87).

In our last chapter, we discussed Verse 22, where Jesus said,

"When you make an eye in the place of an eye and a hand in the place of a hand, and a foot in the place of a foot, and an image in the place of an image, then you will enter the Kingdom." One way to understand this cryptic saying is that we cannot actually use any knowledge handed to us. I cannot use an eye or a hand given to me by another, I can only use the eyes or hands that are fashioned from my own body. Just so, I cannot use knowledge handed to me by another – book knowledge – but only that knowledge which comes from my own experience, that which "emerges from within," as Eckhart says. Thus it will do no good to simply be told that all is One. I must experience that oneness, I must know it for myself to be true. But how does one gain such knowledge?

Sudden or gradual enlightenment

When I was a child growing up in an evangelical church, every church service would end with an altar call. An endurance test for children, the altar call came at the end of a forty-five minute sermon, and could itself last twenty minutes. During the altar call the minister would plead with those in the congregation who were not "saved" to come forward and "receive Jesus." Anyone who did was promised instantaneous salvation. A recitation of a magical formula (the "sinners prayer") guaranteed one a place in heaven quicker than one could blink.

When I grew up and began exploring mainline protestant and catholic churches, I discovered a very different model. Rather than instant salvation, they preached a more gradual process, in which one became a Christian more by exposure and osmosis than a momentary decision.

These two poles are not unique to contemporary Christianity, of course. Among the Zen Buddhist schools, there is a similar divergence of opinion. The Rinzai school, for instance, champions instant enlightenment, while the Soto school favors a process of gradual enlightenment.

Clearly both are valuable schools of thought and salvific for different people. The Gospel of Thomas, however, is firmly in the gradual enlightenment camp. Jesus is quite clear that saving knowledge will not fall out of the sky unannounced, taking us by surprise. We are not simply passive recipients, but can only receive this knowing as a result of our own active pursuit. Enlightenment might be a gift, but we will have to work to prepare ourselves to receive it, for as we shall see, it is not easy to receive such knowledge, and if we have not done the work ahead of time, we cannot help but to reject it.

In verse five Jesus says, "Know what is before your face, and that which is hidden will be revealed to you. For there is nothing hidden which will not be revealed." He is describing a two-part movement, an active motion on our part which will be followed by an action on God's part, of which we are the passive recipients. He promises that the mysteries of the universe will be revealed to us – an intriguing promise indeed – but in order to receive such treasure we must first do something very difficult: to see that which is before our very eyes.

OR that which occurs before – not in front of – our sensory organs (in a face)

The active movement: mindfulness

This is much harder to do than it sounds. For instance, do you remember the color of the eyes of the person who waited on you when you bought your coffee this morning? Do you know the license plate number of the person ahead of you in your last traffic jam? Can you recall the details of everything your spouse related to you just before you went to bed last night?

Most of us might remember one or another of these, but it would be rare indeed if we could remember them all, or indeed all the other millions of details we barely notice. Of course, from a psychological perspective, this is as it should be. We have to skip over some details, block some things out in order to focus on that which is truly important. But this is Jesus' point: what we think is important and what Heaven considers important may be two very different things. For Jesus, the small things we consider of no consequence are of equal importance to those things to which we pay close attention.

How can we hope to reach enlightenment – sudden, universal comprehension – if we cannot even recall the name of the receptionist where we work? Yet this person is just as important in the sight of Heaven as our boss.

We're not good at noticing, unfortunately. We pass right by people in the most desperate need, yet they do not even register. So long as such people escape our attention, enlightenment will likewise elude us. How do we "know what is before" our face?

Through much hard work and practice. We have to train our brains not to screen out that which does not concern us. All things concern us, whether we understand why or not. We must disengage the "glossing" mechanism that blinds us to 90% of our environment.

Jesus never gave us a method for "noticing the present moment," but the Buddha taught that this can be achieved through a practice of "mindfulness." As he says in the Dhammapada, "The wise man who by mindfulness conquers thoughtlessness is as one who, free from sorrows, ascends the palace of wisdom and there, from its high terrace, sees those in sorrow below; even as a wise strong man on the holy mountain might behold the many unwise far down below on the plain" (2:28).

Zen Buddhists practice mindfulness by a form of medidation they call "zazen," or "just sitting." To sit zazen yourself, try sitting cross-legged with a straight spine with your eyes open (this will help you stay awake). Once you are comfortable, pay close attention to your breath – notice it coming in, notice it going out. Try to be completely aware of your breathing. This is not easy, as we are usually not conscious of it at all, just as we are not conscious of most of the things around us. While you are breathing, thoughts, fears, and images will inevitably arise in your imagination. This is normal and not to be discouraged. Unlike other forms of meditation, where one tries to banish all thoughts or attempts to reach a mystical state, in zazen one simply sits with what is. When a thought arises, acknowledge it, and then visualize picking it up and moving it to a shelf near your right hand. You know it is there, you are fully aware of it, but do not let it dominate your attention to the exclusion of anything else in your body, mind, or environment. Do the same with feelings: acknowledge them, and gently set them aside, returning your focus to your breath. If a fear emerges, it, too, can be acknowledged, and set aside.

When I am sitting zazen, people can talk, walk, or even run around me. The dog can lick my face without disturbing me, because I am not trying to be anywhere else. I am not trying to avoid the dog or my thoughts or feelings or the neighbor's boom box upstairs or the kid on the skateboard going up and down the street. Instead I am attempting to be *with* all of it. To be *present with* all of it. I do not want to banish any of it, or escape it, or block it out. I want to hold it all, to see it all, experience it all simultaneously. I am trying to shut off the filters that narrow my focus to only my thoughts, or only the dog, or only the music playing. But to experience them all simultaneously is an onslaught to the senses and the brain, and when I am able to do it, I feel like I catch a glimpse of what the universe must be like for God: who, if Thomas is right, is able to be fully present to the whole of Creation.

Though zazen is a practice borrowed from another tradition, it is very effective for achieving what Jesus is asking us to do. The constant chatter of the mind and the unquenchable desire of the ego must be harnessed and quieted before we can be fully present to those sensations within us that are more subtle, and those things outside of us that do not immediately concern our ego. In verse 35, Jesus said, "There is no way a person can enter into the house of a strong man and take him by force, unless he first ties [the strong man's] hands. Then he can loot the house." If we want to find the treasure of enlightenment, we must first learn to control that "strong man" within us.

Some people don't like meditation because they think it is boring, but when we are able to actually *be with* everything that is going on around us, we are more likely to be overwhelmed by experience than we are to be bored. There is *too much* input, rather than not enough. Even in a quiet grove, where at first glance it appears nothing is happening, when we are able to be truly present we find that there is more going on than we can comfortably assimilate.

But comfort is not the point. Effort is the first stage of this journey, and a willingness to make this effort is essential. Not everyone is happy with this arrangement, of course. In verse 91, Jesus' disciples entreat him, saying, "Tell us who you are, so that we may believe in you."

Jesus' followers want to take the easy way out: just *tell us* what is true, *tell us* what to believe. But Jesus knows that there is no shortcut to enlightenment. You can't get there by just believing something or another, or even by believing *in* someone, even him. Martin Luther in the Reformation taught that one is saved not by works but by faith alone, and the whole of the Protestant movement has followed suit, despite the ironic esteem with which our culture holds the "Protestant work ethic."

But the Jesus of Thomas would not have agreed with this at all. His disciples have to *do the work*, and nobody likes to work. Instead of indulging their preference for faith over works, however, Jesus mildly admonishes them, saying, "You read the face of the heavens and the earth, and yet you did not recognize the One who was in your presence; and you do not know how to read the present moment."

In other words, even the wise men and women, the religious authorities, and those who know the movements of the stars do not see that all is One. They do not see the fullness of reality before their very noses, so how can they lead others to it? Jesus' implication is clear. If you want to be enlightened, you must do more than simply map out the important things, you must be fully present with the insignificant as well. In fact, you must be present with all of it. You must be *fully* present, and therefore, everything that distracts us from being fully present should be tempered. Worries have their place, but they should not consume us; loved ones concern us but we should not lose ourselves in them; wine makes the heart glad, but drunkenness blinds us even to the obvious; leadership is necessary, but an obsession with power will destroy us.

Being able to fully read the present moment means that even those things which are dear to us must be held with a degree of indifference, and those things which repulse us must be held with some degree of respect. This is putting Oneness into practice, translating the head knowledge of our unity with all things into the heart knowledge that only comes when we truly *can* hold all things with equal reverance. And this takes hard work and practice.

The passive movement: revelation

If we can achieve mindfulness, and truly "know what is before our face," Jesus promises that "that which is hidden will be revealed" to us. This second movement is not ours, but God's, of which we are the passive recipient. Although it has no doubt happened to some, most of us should not expect that our eyes will suddenly be opened and we will instantly receive the gift of enlightenment. Instead, this revelation, or "unveiling" is a process, too, and even though it happens to us, we must by necessity deal with the content of this revelation. This can be harder than the mindfulness practice, because often the things that are revealed to us are things we do not want to see, cannot now accept, and will fight against with everything we are. For revelation inevitably involves the stripping away of all of our hard-won illusions, the lies we tell even to ourselves to help us get by, the lies we tell to others to keep our poor hearts safe.

But once again, Jesus is not concerned with safety. Thomas tells the other disciples, "If I said to you even one of the things he told me, you would all take up stones and throw them at me...." The things that are revealed to us are often hard to bear, let alone relate. No one wants to hear they are not who they thought they were. All of the things we believe about ourselves are lies. We are not who we thought we were. We are not this ego, this bag of flesh and bones. When our revelation is complete we will be able to say with Jesus, "I am the All, from me all things have emerged and to me all things have been revealed." Anything less is illusion.

Buddhism speaks of the ego as our False Face. It is not who we really are, though we pretend it is, even to ourselves. The universe, the All, the One, however, is our True Face. It is this True Face that we hope will be revealed to us gradually by walking this path. But the illusion that we are our False Face does not die easy. In verse

37, Jesus' disciples said to him, "When will you be unveiled to us, and when will we look upon you?" Jesus answered, "When you strip yourselves naked without being ashamed, and take your garments and put them under your feet and trample them like little children, then you will look upon the child of the One Who Lives, and you will become fearless."

Again, the disciples are focused on Jesus, which is absolutely the wrong locus for their attention: "When will you be unveiled to us...?" Instead, it is the disciples who need to be unveiled. Their illusions must be stripped from them like their clothes, their false identities must be trampled underfoot. And the child of the One Who Lives? It is not Jesus (or not only Jesus), but it is in fact the disciples themselves as they truly are. Meister Eckhart entreated his own students to do the same when he wrote, "I advise you to let your own 'being you' sink away and melt into God's 'being God.' In this way your 'you' and God's 'his,' will become a completely one 'my.' And you will come to know his changeless existence and his nameless nothingness" (46). This process is terrifying, yet if we can endure such knowledge, fear will be banished along with our myriad illusions.

Jesus speaks to this again in a verse that is echoed in the canonical gospels. Jesus said in verse 26, "You see the speck in your brother's eye, but you do not see the log in your own eye. When you remove the log from your own eye, then you will be able to see well enough to remove the speck from your brother's eye."

We typically read this as an admonishment against judging others, and indeed there are echoes of this interpretation in various Buddhist texts as well – as the Buddha said in the *Dhammapada*, "If a man sees the sins of others and forever thinks of their faults, his own sins increase forever and far off is he from the end of his faults" (18:253).

But in light of Thomas' teaching, this verse takes on another, deeper meaning. The log in our own eye represents all the illusions that blind us to the essential unity of all things, to who and what we truly are. How can we instruct others unless our own illusions are banished? As Jesus said in verse 34, "If a blind person leads a blind person, they both fall into a ditch."

The message here is clear: we must do our own inner work before we can help others. We all have a huge log to remove from our eyes: the illusion of separateness. We must strip off the lies in which we have clothed ourselves and trample them underfoot before our true nature can be revealed to us. But how does this knowledge come, and how can we prepare for its terrible truths?

Progressive revelation: stages of faith

We can prepare by knowing how the process will unfold, even without specifically knowing ahead of time the content of our revelations. James Fowler is a developmental psychologist who has spent his career studying the process of faith development, or how spiritual growth normally occurs in human experience, regardless of religious tradition.

Fowler's system is complex and baroque, and in my opinion, a little Piaget goes a long way. However, another psychologist, Scott Peck (author of the excellent *The Road Less Travelled*), has simplified Fowler's system, making it much easier to describe and work with. As we shall see, this simplification has deep resonances with ancient wisdom traditions, including the Gospel of Thomas.

Fowler and Peck describe spiritual growth as a developmental process, and most people move through the various stages of faith in a certain order, experiencing similar processes as their journeys unfold.

In Peck's *Different Drum* (New York: Simon & Schuster, 1987), he describes **Stage I** as chaotic and antisocial. Peck sees this as the "unregenerate soul," interested primarily in self-satisfaction. He says that, "most young children and perhaps one in five adults" fall into this stage (p. 150). It is the stage of undeveloped spirituality, where real, self-giving love and sacrifice are rare.

Stage II is formal, institutional faith. In this stage, a person gives over the care of his or her spiritual life to an authority (such as a religious institution, scripture, dogma, or even a certain minister or guru), whereby a person is liberated from chaos, and life is given order, meaning, and purpose. This is a very real salvation in itself, similar to the structure and order the military gives to some, and is appropriate for older children, and many adults. In this stage, the authority acts on behalf of the Divine, and one strives to align one's own will with it. The divine is largely seen as "other," a transcendent being with very clear boundaries regarding conduct and doctrine. Among Christians, all fundamentalists and many Catholics and mainline Protestants fall into this category. Orthodox Jews are also most likely to be Stage II believers, and in fact most religions have conservative wings that fit into this category.

Not everyone will be content with the degree of legalism this stage entails, however. Those who begin to question the institution move into **Stage III**, or skeptical, individual faith. Many Stage III seekers are agnostics, acknowledging that they do not know what ultimate reality is, nor how to approach it. They may read far and wide in the fields of philosophy and world religion, and may begin to piece together an eclectic and individual spirituality that is uniquely theirs. This "rebel" period puts them at odds with most institutions, and Stage III seekers are generally suspicious of organized religion of any kind. Many people will find a lifelong home in this stage, creating meaning in their lives as activists, humanists, or social reformers.

But many will find that their skeptical journey brings them back around to the truths to be found in faith traditions. **Stage IV** Mystics are in love with the Mystery that pervades the universe, the ineffable Divinity which cannot be named, comprehended, or quantified. Mystics value religious tradition, but hold its institutions lightly, investing in the vision of Divinity offered by a tradition, but not necessarily in the trappings. Dogma and discipline may be useful fodder for contemplation, but for mystics, all of this is subordinate to the essential Mystery which transcends the human, cultural "clothes" it is dressed in by any given faith. Mystics see all things as connected; all beings, all places, all times meet and are at One in the Mystery.

As Scott Peck writes, Mystics "love mystery, in dramatic contrast to those in Stage II, who need simple, clear-cut dogmatic structures and have little taste for the unknown and unknowable. While Stage

IV men and women will enter religion in order to approach mystery, people in Stage II, to a considerable extent, enter religion in order to escape from it. Thus there is the confusion of people entering not only into religion but into the same religion – and sometimes the same denomination – not only for different motives but for totally opposite motives" (p. 154).

Discovering Fowler's system was life-changing for me, because it helped me see that I was not simply a hell-bound heretic, but was engaged in a process that was both normal and, perhaps for someone of my inquisitive disposition, inevitable. Fowler's research has been ground-breaking for those seeking to understand the mechanics of spiritual growth, yet for all of his original research, the model is far from new. It is, in fact, very ancient indeed.

The Gnostic Christians likewise divided the spiritual journey into four stages, each of which corresponds exactly to Peck's adaptation of Fowler's system. The Gnostics did not speak about faith as a developmental process, but instead divided people into four categories, with the assumption that people can and do move from one category to the next, much as Fowler and Peck describe.

First, there are the **Hylics**. These are those people whom the Gnostics believed possessed no spiritual wisdom, and thus have no hope of salvation. They are doomed to perpetually reincarnate on this prison-planet. Similar to those of Peck's Stage I, they are unregenerate, live in a chaotic inner world, and have no relationship with the heavenly powers.

Second are the **Psychics**. These are the "conventional" Christians who follow the teachings of the institutional, Pauline church, analogous to Peck's Stage II believers. They have partial knowledge, but they worship the demiurge, a flawed lesser god who created this universe, and have no knowledge of the true God who dwells in the world of light beyond this universe. They have a partial salvation, for though they know the words of Jesus, they do not correctly understand them. Their lives have order and the illusion of meaning, but they still are doomed to perpetual reincarnations.

Next are the **Pneumatics**, which fall into two categories: those with head knowledge of the truth, and those who have truly experienced enlightenment. Those with head knowledge have been brought into the inner circle of the Gnostic community, and have been told the great secret: the god they have worshipped all their lives is not the real God at all, but merely a flawed, malevolent pretender to the throne. This world they enjoy is not a good creation at all, but a place of suffering, torture, and perpetual imprisonment, as our souls continually reincarnate here with little hope of escape. These are similar to Peck's Stage III, for armed with this new information they rebel against institutional religion and become suspicious of its leaders and its claims.

Eventually, though, under the guidance of fellow Pneumatics, their head knowledge is transformed by the gift of *gnosis,* the experience of complete knowing, known in the East as *satori,* or enlightenment. Through various rituals which engender altered states of consciousness, these Pneumatics open themselves to divine revelation, and many believed they received it. Like Peck's Stage IV Mystics, Enlightened Pneumatics are able to enjoy their union with the Divine without necessarily being able to describe or explain it. One can only experience such knowledge; words will always fail.

As fascinating as the similarities between Peck's model and the Gnostic model are, more astounding still is the fact that these models are preceded by an even older formulation of this same process, found of course, in the Gospel of Thomas. In verse two, Jesus said, "Let the one who seeks keep on seeking until he finds, and when he finds, he will be troubled, and if he is troubled, he will become surprised, and will become sovereign over all things."

"One who seeks" is he who knows that he does not have the knowledge he requires to navigate this life. Like Peck's Stage I person or the Gnostics' Hylics, a seeker's life is chaotic and void of spiritual guidance. The pain of such chaos is what motivates one to seek.

The seeker eventually "finds" what he or she is looking for. The one who has found an answer is like Peck's Stage II Believer or the Gnostics' Psychics. They have something to cling to, some explanation for the vicissitudes of life.

For the person on the way of Thomas, however, there is little comfort in pat answers. The answers provided inevitable lead only to more questions, for "when he finds, he will be troubled." This step is like Peck's Stage III skeptic or the Gnostics' head-knowledge Pneumatic.

Finally, he or she will "be surprised and will be sovereign over all things." Staying with the questions that arise, not settling for canned answers, bearing the discomfort of not knowing will eventually pay off. This final stage is like Peck's Stage IV Mystic or the Gnostics' Enlightened Pneumatic.

It is significant that the final stage be surprise (which could also be translated "wonder" or "awe") since true enlightenment is unlike anything we can imagine and is beyond the capacity of language to relate. But we will not only be shocked, we will also rule, or be sovereign. Once we know ourselves to be One, then the sovereignty of God is our sovereignty as well, since we and God are One and the same.

The difficulty with developmental systems is that they are inevitably hierarchical. It is assumed that Stage II is somehow better than Stage I (in this case, I believe it is), or that Stage III is better than Stage II (which is certainly not true for some people who need the structure of Stage II to simply survive). This is an argument for another work, but another result of this perceived hierarchy which does concern us is that one gets the idea that spiritual progress using one of these (very similar) models is like climbing a ladder. You take step after step and eventually you get to the top, and you have "made it." You might get the idea that by just following Jesus' plan for spiritual growth in verse two when you get to the "surprised and sovereign" part, you will be fully enlightened.

My experience, however, is that this is not a linear process, but a cyclic one. It is not a ladder to be climbed, but a spiral to be followed around again and again. Each time one journeys through the cycle, one gains a little more knowledge, one becomes a little more enlightened. But the frustrating thing is that the more we know, the more we realized we *don't* know. Each journey through these steps generates more questions and reveals deeper and deeper levels of illusion to be banished, and greater Unity than we dared imagine. Each time we see ways in which we have separated ourselves from God and from others as we discover prejudices and blind spots we did not know we had. Each time around affords us greater and greater freedom.

When I first discovered Peck's system, it was easy to see how I had followed the pattern. A child in Stage I, I had surrendered my life to Christ at eight years old, and grew into Stage II, where I was more or less happy until my early adulthood as a Southern Baptist fundamentalist. After some very painful episodes, I rebelled and discarded the faith of my parents and began to look to other religions for answers in Stage III. Then when I realized that all religions were pointing to the same eternal Source, I entered Stage IV and intended to settle down as a mystical Christian.

I had ended up a convert to the Episcopal Church by this time, and with all the zeal of a convert, I was sure that every other expression of Christianity was inferior, as I had found such intellectual and theological liberation as an Episcopalian.

Though my enlightenment was a true one, after some painful encounters with others who had found their mystical homes in places other than the Episcopal Church, I eventually came to see that I had traded one form of fundamentalism for another. Although the notion of a "liberal fundamentalist" seems oxymoronic, the world is full of them. Indeed, anyone who has been on the spiritual path has probably been one at one time or another just as I was.

This realization began another round of seeking, finding, being troubled, wondering and ruling. And it was certainly not the last time. Each time I spiral through, more of my own blindness is revealed to me, and more truth as well.

The school of Thomas, then, is by no means a "sudden" school of enlightenment. Instead, it is like most things of value in human endeavors: slow, messy, and deliberate. This is most likely a good thing, because only in this way can the revelations be made so that we are not overwhelmed by them and can actually receive and assimilate them. If all knowledge in heaven and earth were suddenly implanted in us, and the horror of all our illusions instantaneously ripped away, I doubt many of us could withstand it. The Jewish scriptures say that Moses had to view God's backside because if he beheld God's face he would surely die. If it is so for someone as great as Moses, it is surely true of me, and unless you are the Dalai Lama, it is probably true of you, too.

Nonetheless, Jesus promises in verse 17, "I will give to you what eyes have never seen, what no ear has heard, what hands have not touched, and what has never arisen in the human heart," but not, thank God, all at once. The Bible tells us that God will not give us more than we have the capacity to bear (1 Cor. 10:13), and I believe this is as true of revelation as it is more mundane burdens.

But where, you might ask, is such a lengthy and painstaking journey taking us? Once layer after layer of illusion is removed from our eyes, what sort of promised land will we behold? Jesus spoke of this more often than perhaps any other teaching. He promises that if we are faithful, if we are willing to do the work, if we can bear the sometimes terrible revelations this path has in store for us, we will eventually enter the Kingdom.

Spiritual exercises

1. If you do not already meditate, try setting aside 15 minutes a day and **practice doing zazen.** Notice what comes up for you – what thoughts, fears, or images emerge while you are sitting. After your session, jot down a list of those things you have put on the shelf during your session. After a while, these little lists of "things on the shelf" will have things to teach us as we notice patterns and the surprising items that sometimes pop up.

2. **Write a short spiritual autobiography,** describing the first time you cycled through Peck's faith stages. (Note: If you have not cycled through at least once, this book would piss you off or utterly bore you too much to even read it). If you have cycled more than once, write about your other cycles as well. This will help you normalize your experience, to see it as a process that everyone can go through if they are determined to work at it, and will also help you recognize the various stages as you cycle through them again and again.

The Kingdom of Heaven has already arrived

In spite of all our feelings of sorrow or well-being
God wants us to understand and know by faith
that we are more truly in heaven than on earth.

– Julian of Norwich (91)

The Kingdom of Heaven may be the most misunderstood part of Jesus' teaching. This is ironic, since it was also one of the most important. How could Jesus' most emphasized teaching be so consistently misrepresented? Part of the reason is that the confusion goes back to Jesus' own day, to a misunderstanding that played an integral part in both his ministry and his death.

When Jesus was ministering in Israel, the Jews were an occupied people. Time and again in their history, the Jewish people had suffered under foreign tyrants. The memory of being slaves in Egypt served as the archetype for their experience of being a conquered people, but this story played itself out again and again through their history. They were later carried away into slavery in Babylon, and had once again been delivered from their oppressors. Centuries later Judas Maccabaeus and his sons led a revolt that threw off the yoke of the Greeks. But by the time of Jesus, the Jews once again found themselves subject to a foreign power. This time it was Rome, whose undisputed might made it difficult to believe that a small band of freedom fighters such as the Maccabees could defeat them.

A mythology had been brewing since the Babylonian captivity, however, that gave the people hope. They looked forward to a Messiah (which means "anointed one" or "king") who would emerge from the Jewish people as a great military leader, greater than Judas Maccabaeus, possessed of divine favor and capable of wielding supernatural power. Under the leadership of this God-given hero, Israel would rouse itself from its occupied sleep, and though hopelessly outnumbered, would face the might of Rome with resolve. And just as the Jews had been delivered from their enemies time and again, against impossible odds, they believed that God would once again miraculously deliver them.

They anticipated defeating Rome, and setting up a new empire with Jerusalem as its capitol. Then all of the nations which had persecuted the Jews throughout history would be called before the throne of Jerusalem to be judged. The Messiah would sit on that throne and rule the world for a thousand years of peace, a reign known as the Kingdom of God, or the Kingdom of Heaven.

It is ironic that the Jews, so long a persecuted people, would fantasize of subduing others, but that is human nature. And the notion of this tiny nation defeating the Roman army and setting up a rival empire of their own was laughable. But the Jews believed that all things were possible with God on their side, and the more oppressed they felt the more they invested in the dream of the Messiah and the Kingdom of God.

The Romans were well aware of this mythology and though they had no doubt that they could easily squash this pesky and unruly nation, they struggled to maintain peace in the region. They kept a sizable force employed in Israel because of the constant unrest. Of course, the visibility and number of troops might have discouraged unripe attempts to throw off the Roman yoke, but it also added fuel to the rebellious fires. It was a vicious circle that threatened to spin out of control at any moment.

The people were eager to be free of Rome, and the anticipation of the Messiah raged like a fever. A party of political radicals known as the Zealots were trying to organize a covert army, so that when the Messiah appeared, there would be troops ready to mobilize beneath his banner. They and many other groups were on the lookout for this Messiah, and they were sure he would arrive at any moment.

It was in this political environment that Jesus began his ministry, and there were many who believed that he might in fact be the one they were waiting for. A lot of the qualities they felt the Messiah must possess were present in him: he was a skilled teacher of righteousness, obviously well-versed in the religious lore of his people. He also had plenty of charisma, and an innate ability to lead. He also did not seem to be in the pocket of the religious authorities who were collaborating with Rome, and seemed, in fact, to oppose them.

The zealots even sent one of their own, Judas Iscariot, to follow Jesus and try to get a read on him: was this the Messiah, the one they were waiting for? Would Jesus raise the slumbering Jewish army and conquer their oppressors? Would he liberate their people and sit on the throne of David to judge the nations?

But Jesus proved to be difficult to read. When questioned about whether he was the Messiah, his answers were ambiguous and noncommittal. Even when asked outright about the coming Kingdom, he was confounding. The Gospel of Thomas records such an exchange, when his disciples ask him, "When will the kingdom arrive?" Jesus answers them, "It is not coming in a way you can see outwardly. No one is going to say, "Look, over there!" or "There it is!" Rather, the Kingdom of the Father is spread out upon the earth, and people do not see it" (113).

To the great disappointment of those looking for a military leader, Jesus seemed completely uninterested in raising an army. He told them instead that the Kingdom of God was not a political state that would someday be established by the sword, but a spiritual reality that was already present for those who knew how to perceive it. It is even now "spread out upon the earth," but invisible to people who are looking for something else.

Christians in later centuries had a different idea of what the Kingdom was. For them, the Kingdom *was* Heaven, the place of eternal rest, bliss, and reward that awaited all faithful Christians in the afterlife. They looked forward to the time when the present worlds would pass away, and a new Heaven and a new earth took their place. But the Gospel of Thomas anticipates this interpretation, and the Jesus of Thomas likewise debunks it. His disciples ask him, "When will the dead find their rest? And when will the new world arrive?" But he answered them, "That day you look for has already come. But you, you do not recognize it" (51).

Once again, Jesus is shattering the hopes of those who look for some dramatic future event that will make sense of all the troubles and tribulations of this life. In both cases Jesus rejects the notion that deliverance is to come in some future time or in some future life. Deliverance is now, the Kingdom is here, but his followers are simply blind to it.

So what is the Kingdom and how do we see it? Jesus gives us a hint in one of the most humorous verses in Thomas: Jesus said, "If those who lead you say to you, 'Look, the kingdom is in the sky,' then the birds will get there before you do. If they say to you, 'It is in the sea,' the fish will get there first. Instead, the kingdom inside you – and it is outside of you. When you come to know yourselves, then you will be known, and you will realize that you are the children of the living Father. If, however, you do not come to know yourselves, then you dwell in poverty, and you are that poverty" (3).

Because the Kingdom is a mystical reality, there is no physical place one can point to, and Jesus implies that any religious leader who tries to do so is full of baloney. The Buddha echoes this teaching in the *Dhammapada* when he said, "There is no path in the sky...a monk must find the inner path" (18:255).

No one can simply show someone the Kingdom – the Kingdom is a place we must all find for ourselves. Not even Jesus could point it out to his followers. The best he could do was abide in the Kingdom himself and offer guidance as to how they might gain access. As he told them in verse three, the Kingdom is "inside" them and "outside" them – familiar to us from chapter one and our discussion of the eradication of duality. The Kingdom is a place where such dualisms do not exist or have been transcended. He goes on to say that "When you come to know yourselves, then you will be known, and you will realize that you are the children of the living Father." The Kingdom is the habitation of those who, as we discussed in chapter two, have discerned their true self from their false self, and to whom their real identity has been revealed.

The Kingdom then, is not a political nation or a heavenly reward, but is the state of unitive consciousness we enjoy when we are fully present with all things. It is easy to understand the *idea* of unitive consciousness, and through successive revelations, our capacity for uniting the many dualisms we inhabit can increase, but to actually *live* in a state of undifferentiated awareness is another thing altogether. It is extraordinarily difficult, and requires much patience and practice. But it is its own reward, and until we gain access to this blessed realm, we dwell in a poverty of our own making.

This is the task of the one who walks the Way of Thomas: to realize the oneness of all things, and the gradual revelation of the staggering scope of this oneness. All of this is simply preparation for life in the Kingdom.

This is more a process of unlearning than it is learning something new. Unitive consciousness is not only our true nature, it is our original experience of the world. As infants, we come mewling into the world enveloped in the All. The unitive experience of the womb does not pass for some time. The infant does not know he or she is a separate being from his or her mother, or indeed, from the rest of the universe. The infant is One.

Remember the ego-wall we have to build to make our way in the world? (We discussed this in Chapter One.) The ego-wall is a learned defense mechanism, it is not who we really are. The Jesus of Thomas calls us to unlearn this defense, to break down the internal barrier by which we perceive ourselves to be separate from everything else. We must return to a state, not only of innocence, but of oneness.

Jesus speaks of this in verse twenty-two, as he is watching some babies being nursed. He said to his disciples, "These little ones who are being suckled are like those who go into the Kingdom." Those little ones do not perceive a difference between themselves and the breast they suck at, or the clothes they are swaddled in. Both Mommie and themselves are simply lost in the All. Jesus said, "A person of great age will not hesitate to ask a little child seven days old about the place of Life, and he will live, for all those who are first will become last, and they will become a single one" (4).

The delicious irony of verse four is that the baby is actually wiser than the old man, since it has nothing to unlearn. Pride and common sense prevent us from seeking wisdom from infants, but the spiritual journey is filled with such paradoxes. Jesus promises that if we can put away our objections and sit at the feet of the infant as our teacher, thus allowing the "first to become last," we will find the Life we seek, as the distinction between the infant and ourselves melts away and we become "a single one."

This is the true meaning of being "born again" in St John's Gospel. Nichodemus comes to visit Jesus by night and asks what he must do to gain eternal life. Jesus tells him he must be born again. Nichodemus objects, "How can I enter my mother's womb a second time?" But Jesus isn't talking about physical birth. By becoming as an infant, reclaiming our unitive consciousness, we are indeed born again. We are born into an essentially alien world; one we once knew, and must come to know again, if we are to gain eternal life.

There is a Buddhist story that tells of a little fish that hears about the ocean. He thinks it must be a marvelous place, and he goes out to find it. He swims for many miles, yet he never finds this ocean. Eventually, he encounters a wise and elderly fish who informs him that he is already in the ocean, and he does not need to search any longer. The little fish is overwhelmed, and enlightened.

Just like this little fish, we grow up believing that God is "out there" somewhere, but the truth is we are swimming in God, and we simply do not know it. We are already living in the Kingdom, but if we are not aware of it, what good does it do us? "The Kingdom of the Father is spread out upon the earth, and people do not see it."

So how do we learn to live in the Kingdom? How do we transform a moment of insight into a way of life? The Way of Thomas is no lazy man's path to enlightenment: living in the Kingdom takes

practice. In verse 98, Jesus said, "The kingdom of the father is like
a man who wanted to kill a powerful man. In his house, he drew a
sword, and stuck it into the wall so that he might know whether he
had the skill to do it. Then he killed the powerful man."

One way to understand this enigmatic verse is to view the
"powerful man" as the ego (a powerful guy if there ever was one).
The ego is not simply going to curl up and die at the first whiff of
mysticism – in fact it is going to go out kicking and screaming the
whole way. It will do anything to maintain its illusion of reality and
control. Killing the powerful man takes practice.

Brother Lawrence was a Roman Catholic monk who lived about
300 years ago. He was crippled, not esteemed to be a great intellect,
and worked for most of his life as a dishwasher in his monastery.
Due to his great desire for intimacy with God, he began to talk to
God all the time, as one would talk to a close friend. Lawrence's
biographer, Joseph de Beaufort, wrote of him, "In the beginning,
Brother Lawrence declared that a little effort was needed to form the
habit of continuously conversing with God, telling Him everything
that was happening. But after a little careful practice, God's love
refreshed him, and it all became quite easy" (11). Brother Lawrence's
book *The Practice of the Presence of God* is a classic of Western spiritual
literature, and has been used for centuries by people seeking the
Kingdom. Like Lawrence, we, too, can live perpetually in God's
presence, aware of our oneness with all things.

Though "the practice of the presence of God" has a great ring
to it, today we more often speak of "mindfulness practice," a term
borrowed from Buddhism. The mind (and the ego which inhabits
it) is easily bored if it is not being gratified in some way, and so
our attention automatically shifts to a fantasy about the future
or a memory of the past, anything to avoid the mundanity of the
present. But through hard work we can re-train the mind to stay
in the present. As we saw in our discussion of zazen, the present
isn't really boring at all – in fact there is always much more going
on than we can possibly assimilate. We are simply blocking most of
it out. But by doing zazen, or walking meditation, or by constant
conversation with God, or by some other practice, we can teach

ourselves to stay in the present. As Brother Lawrence found, it is quite difficult at first, but if we persist, it does get easier.

This practice is very important, because the Kingdom does not exist in the past or the future. So long as one is inhabiting the past or the future, one is absent from the Kingdom. The Kingdom exists only in the present, and we get to choose whether or not we want to live there.

What is it like to live in the Kingdom?

Once we put in the effort, and learn to live in the Kingdom, what will we find there? How is life different, what are its ramifications? Needless to say, living in the Kingdom is a radical re-orientation, and there are few aspects of life that are untouched by the move.

We have everything we need. Once we get used to living in the present, we stop fretting over the past or worrying about the future. This means we stop obsessing over having enough money, or about our physical security. After all, if we *are* everything, then everything is ours. Meister Eckhart says as much when he writes, "All are sent or no one is sent, into all or into nothing. For in the kingdom of heaven, all is in all, all is one, and all is ours. And, in the kingdom of heaven, everything is in everything else. All is one and all is ours. We are all in all, as God is all in all" (114).

Jesus' words in Matthew's gospel make much more sense in such a unitive context, when he says,

> Don't worry about your life, about whether you have enough
> to eat or drink, or clothes to wear. Is life not more than food
> and clothing? Look at the birds, they neither sow nor reap
> or store in barns, because your heavenly father feeds them.
> And aren't you more important than the birds? Can all your
> worries add a single moment to your life? And why worry
> about clothing? Look at the lilies, how they grow in the field.
> They do not work, nor do they spin thread, yet Solomon
> in all of his glory was not adorned such as they are. And if
> God cares so much for flowers, which are here today and

gone tomorrow, will he not also care for you? You have so
little faith! So do not worry about having enough food or
drink or clothes. The gentiles are so concerned about these
things, yet your Father knows that you need them, and he
will give you all that you need from day to day if you make
the Kingdom of Heaven your chief concern. So don't worry
about tomorrow, for tomorrow will bring its own worries.
Today's troubles are enough for today (6:25-34).

If we are not practicing unitive consciousness, then this kind of
living requires radical trust, a faith that God will provide for us. But
if we are truly living in the Kingdom, faith doesn't enter into it. We
are not worrying about the future precisely because we are too busy
living in the present to be aware of the future. Unlike Matthew's
Jesus, the Jesus of Thomas never asks us for faith, but to simply be
as present as he is present, to know the world as he does, to be one
with it as he is.

Note that Jesus is talking about the bare necessities of life in this
passage. He is not talking about SUV's, high-definition television
sets, gameboys, or weekend flats in Marin County. The promise is
that we will have everything we need, not everything we want. But
if we are truly living in the present, we are not daydreaming about
what we do not have. Being in the Kingdom leads us to a way of life
that impacts creation lightly, does not hoard wealth, does not waste
natural resources. The bumper sticker that reads, "Live simply that
others may simply live" contains wisdom congruent with Jesus'
teaching. When we are living in the Kingdom, we have all that is
necessary, even if we have nothing at all.

We bring peace to all beings. If we are not striving after selfish
accumulation, or accruing power for ourselves, if we are focused
on simply being, then we are content to simply let others be as well.
We do not view people or animals as resources to be exploited, or as
expendable pawns in our wargames. If we have everything we need,
we do not need to defraud our neighbors out of their possessions;
if we do not grasp after power, we do not need to regulate their
behavior or coerce them to do our bidding. Living in the Kingdom,

we find peace for ourselves, and we can extend that peace to others, not by demanding that they see things as we do, but by simply not expecting anything of them. Once we learn to simply be, we can let others be as well.

This creates a peace of mind that is infectious, for not only do we enjoy this peace, but everyone we come in contact with can enjoy it as well. It is a peace that radiates out and touches all that we touch. This may seem like a small thing, and it is often hard to see how an action in our personal life can effect a change in our common life, or our global life. Yet when Jesus' disciples say to him, "Tell us what the Kingdom of Heaven is like," he answered them, saying, "It is like a grain of mustard – the smallest of all the seeds. When, however, it falls to the earth and is given care, it sends out great branches to be shade for the birds of the sky" (20).

The seed of peace that mindfulness plants in us has an effect on the world that is often difficult to fathom. Just as rage escalates from person to person, and what begins as an annoyance can spin out of control into a crisis for a whole community or even a nation, so peace can be likewise infectious. But while rage is uncomfortable and easily noticed, peace is often invisible to us. This is because, unlike human beings – who are exiles from the Kingdom – nature is a permanent resident. All plants, rocks, and animals (all who are not self-reflexive, that is) live in the Kingdom full-time, as Jesus points out regarding the birds and the lilies in the passage just quoted above from Matthew's Gospel. None of them spend their time obsessing over the past or the future, but live fully present in the here-and-now. The Kingdom is indeed "spread out upon the earth, but people do not see it." Jesus invites us not only to see it, but to join the rest of the created order in living there. The peace that results is not only a gift to us, but to creation itself, not least because we are far less likely to disturb its peace if we are content with what we have.

Tolerant of all peoples. When we are content to simply let things be what they are, we feel less need to coerce or change them. This includes people, too. While the other rabbis were focused on which people were okay to associate with and which were not, Jesus simply ate dinner with everybody.

One day while Jesus was at dinner with a fellow Pharisee, a prostitute came and anointed Jesus' feet with oil, and dried them with her hair (Luke 7:36). The Pharisee was horrified, and told Jesus, "How can you let her do that? Do you know how valuable that oil is? You could sell it and give the money to the poor!" But what the Pharisee really objected to was that Jesus allowed himself to be touched by such an untouchable.

But Jesus turned his rebuke aside, saying, "You will always have the poor with you, but I am here right now. You did not wash my feet, you did not anoint them with sweet-smelling ointment. Who are you to rebuke her?"

In verse 57, Jesus says "The kingdom of the father is like a man who had good seed. In the night his enemy came and mixed weeds among the good seed. The man did not let them pull up the weeds. He told them, 'Don't pull up the weeds or you might pull up the grain with it. When harvest comes, the weeds will be plain, and they can be pulled up and burned.'"

The Kingdom is self-selective. You can choose whether to live in it or not. Those who dwell there do not need to worry about who is grain and who is a weed, for all is one. But when death comes, those who have not discovered oneness will indeed be lost to the illusion of separation. This illusion is a vicious cycle that feeds on and perpetuates itself. This is not a judgement from without, imposed by some supreme being, but a self-judgement that is the inevitable result of buying into an illusory reality. As Jesus says in verse 3. "If you do not come to know yourselves, then you dwell in poverty, and you are that poverty."

In the Kingdom, however, there are no insiders or outsiders. There are no good people and bad people. There is no "us" and "them." There is only "us." The division of people into "acceptable" and "unacceptable" is a false dualism, the answer to which is to make the two into one. Just as Jesus invited his host to see the world in a new way, we too are invited to live in the present, to enjoy the presence of divinity wherever we are, to honor the divine in everyone we meet.

Again, Jesus' admonition, "Whatsoever you do to the least of these my brethren, you do it unto me," is meant literally from the perspective of the Thomas Gospel. The prostitute *is* Jesus, just as every prostitute is us. Everyone is *us*. How can we possibly discriminate? As the *Tao Te Ching* asks, "Can you embrace wholeness and not be fragmented?" (10). In the Kingdom, everyone is equal, everyone is acceptable, everyone is welcome.

Things are radically re-prioritized. Once we become citizens of the Kingdom, all of our previous alliances, identities, and affiliations become moot. Once, when Jesus was teaching, his disciples interrupted him, saying, "Your brothers and your mother are standing outside." But instead of rushing out to speak with them, he took the opportunity to use the situation to teach. He said to them, "Those here who do the will of my father, these are my brothers and my mother; it is they who will go into the kingdom of my father" (99).

There is a whiff of dualism detectable here in the Thomas Gospel, between those who have gained entrance to the Kingdom and those who have not. We might infer from this verse that Jesus esteemed those who achieved unitive consciousness over those who had not. Whether this was actually so, we will never know, but it is not consistent with the balance of his teaching in this Gospel. Perhaps this verse reflects the bias of those disciples who first compiled these teachings. Nonetheless, since this verse occurs both in Thomas and in the canonical record (Mark 3:31-34), we can assume that it is an ancient and well-regarded teaching.

From the canonical perspective, the verse is usually interpreted to mean that once one has become a Christian, one gains a new family, to whom one owes a greater allegiance than one does to one's biological family. But from the perspective of the teachings of the Thomas school, a deeper meaning may be divined.

Those in the Kingdom are aware that everyone is, in fact, them. For such a person, a homeless man he or she has never met is just as close a relation as the sibling he or she grew up with. I may not know the homeless man quite as well as I know my sister, but the homeless man is no less a part of me than she is.

And if that homeless man is a resident of the Kingdom, as well (a notion not to be dismissed, since such a person may indeed be closer to a mystical awareness than one who is "successful" in the eyes of the world, and spends all of his or her time chasing after promissory notes), then it may be that a greater mutuality and intimacy is possible with him than with one's own family members.

But family ties are not the only allegiances that are re-prioritized once one decides to take up residence in the Kingdom. Every allegiance becomes meaningless, indeed every category into which one could put anyone becomes arbitrary: conservative or liberal, gay or straight, good or bad, domestic or foreign, married or single, saved or lost, smart or dumb, Catholic or Protestant, rich or poor, crazy or sane, etc. These distinctions exist only in our minds, and are as illusory as our own ego-identity.

The greatest evils have been perpetrated on the basis of ideas alone, "things" which have absolutely no reality in the phenomenal world beyond the power we give them with our imaginations. The Nazis murdered 6 million Jews based on the illusion that they themselves were a superior race, a notion that existed only in their own inflated self-regard. Religious wars the world over have been fought over opposing points of dogma which have no more reality in the physical world than the Easter Bunny.

The Way of Thomas sees through all such illusion, and honors all beings as equally precious. When Jesus said, "Love your brother like your own soul. Guard him like the pupil of your eye" (25), he is not referring to his flesh-and-blood sibling, but to everyone, because everyone *is* your own soul.

For residents in the Kingdom, there are no Democrats or Republicans, no Americans or Canadians, no Christians or Jews, no respecting of persons beyond simple being. The old allegiances we once felt, the esteeming of some to the exclusion of others, simply melt away into the One that we truly are, without distinction or favoritism.

The Buddhist scriptures echo this teaching, saying, "Just as the great rivers, on reaching the great ocean, lose their former names and identities and are reckoned simply as the great ocean, so do followers lose their former names and clans and become sons of the Buddha's clan" (Vinaya, *Cullavagga* 9.I.4).

As residents of the Kingdom, all rivers, however different they may have seemed to us in our former lives, disappear into the great ocean of being.

It can transform the world. This teaching not only changes us, but changes the world around us as well. When we start living in the Kingdom, we treat people differently. As the ancient Hebrew prophets said, "The valleys shall be exalted and the mountains made low." Once unitive consciousness has really been achieved, we treat the famous and infamous exactly alike. The prince and the pauper are held in equal esteem. Of course, this both shocks those in the valleys and pisses off those who live on the mountains. People with power expect to be treated differently than those who have none. Yet, as Jesus shows us, the poor are as worthy of our love and respect as the rich. Likewise the insane, the fallen, and the outsider.

When Jesus went home with Zacchaeus to eat dinner with him (Luke 19:1-10), people were shocked. How dare Jesus share a table with a tax-collector, a thief, a Roman collaborator, a traitor to his people? Yet precisely because Jesus treated him with respect and esteem, Zacchaeus' world was shaken from top to bottom. Zacchaeus had expected scorn – which he was quite used to enduring – but when he received love instead, he was undone, and transformed. He gave back the money he had stolen from people, with interest, and he vowed to do his job fairly from then on.

Likewise, when we treat everyone with equal esteem, we shake up the consensus paradigm. Those at the top are taken down a peg and given a glimpse of their own relative insignificance, while those at the bottom are raised to their feet and are shown their own inestimable worth.

In verse 96, Jesus says, "The kingdom of the father is like a woman who took a little bit of leaven, hid it within some dough, and made it into huge loaves of bread. He who has ears should listen!" Unitive insight is itself the leaven; once we have truly internalized it, and can live oriented to its reality, it transforms our world just as yeast transforms the dough. We grow large inside, beyond the petty divisions that once ordered our world.

Conclusion

The Kingdom is some of the most sought-after real estate in history. People have spent their lives and fortunes searching for it, armies have battled for it, religious leaders have built their empires upon it. And all for nothing, because residence in the Kingdom is free and open to all. It is not coming in some future time, it is here. It is not in a faraway afterlife, it is here.

Religious leaders have misunderstood the Kingdom ever since Jesus' own time, and there is no shortage of misdirection now. Even those talking about the Kingdom are clueless about it. Yet Jesus said, "The kingdom of the father is like a woman carrying a jar full of meal. While she was walking on a road far away, the handle of the jar broke, and the meal emptied out after her upon the road. She didn't notice that anything was wrong, and when she entered her house she put the jar down and discovered it was empty" (97).

Many people think they have the Kingdom sealed up in a jar, their own personal possession. But as Jesus illustrates, the Kingdom of the Father is spread out upon the earth, but people do not notice it; not even those who do the spreading!

The Kingdom is no one's possession unless it is everyone's. There are no insiders, no outsiders. There are no damned, there are no saved. There is no *us*, no *them*. There are simply people who choose to live in the Kingdom and those who do not. Where will you choose to live?

Spiritual exercises

1. **Practice the Presence of God.** Using Brother Lawrence's method, practice being conscious of God's presence continually by talking to the Divine throughout your day. Do it out loud when you can. As Lawrence instructs, you don't have to say anything profound; just describe to God what you are doing as you do it, along with any thoughts and feelings that emerge. Do it for several days until you can sustain awareness of God's presence even when not talking.

2. **Practice walking meditation.** This is a way to further expand your awareness. Choose a quiet spot to walk in, and focus your attention on your breath, just as in zazen. Then step very slowly, being fully aware of everything going on inside and outside you. Be fully present with every step, enjoy the whole process: touching toe, shifting weight, standing full upon the foot, lifting weight, etc. Be aware of God's presence while you do this, as well.

You can escape death by making a simple shift in perception

When we say "God is eternal" we
mean: God is eternally young.
God is ever green, ever verdant, ever flowering.
Every action of God is new, for he makes all things new.
God is the newest thing there is; the youngest thing there is.
God is the beginning and if we are united
to him we become new again.

– Meister Eckhart (32)

The Gospel of Thomas begins, in the very first verse, with a promise: "Whoever happens upon the meaning of these words will not taste death." It is safe to say that the Thomas Christians took these words literally, and believed that the wisdom in this book, if it could be decoded and internalized, would impart immortality.

The spectre of death is a major concern not just for the Thomas Christians, but for all human beings. We are terrified by the thought of our impending deaths. We alone, among all the animals, suffer the knowledge that one day our lives will end. Although all creatures suffer, human beings are blessed and cursed with self-reflexive knowledge that may in fact be the greatest form of suffering.

Thus, death is not only a problem in itself (in that our lives will undoubtedly one day come to an end), the problem is compounded, because the fantasy of future suffering and death distracts us from being present to the here-and-now.

While later Christianity would focus on sin as the main problem in human living, early Christianity saw death as the real culprit. The Thomas Christians shared this concern, as seen in Verse 60. Jesus and the disciples are watching a Saramaritan carrying a lamb. Jesus asks them why he has it, and they answer him, "So that he might kill it and eat it." He said to them, "He will not eat it while it is alive; rather if he kills it, it becomes a corpse." They said, "He cannot do it, otherwise." He said to them, "You yourselves should seek after a place of peace so that you will not become corpses and be eaten yourselves."

The graphic nature of this verse shows the revulsion that the author of this verse had towards death, and a recognition of the cycle of life: of birth, eating, death, and being eaten. But Jesus hints in this verse that there is a way to beat death, to avoid the fate of becoming a corpse and being eaten by worms. That way is to find the "place of peace." We will discuss exactly how to do this later, but for now, it is important to see that this problem of death was just as immediate for Jesus' original hearers as it is for us today. Perhaps more so. I know people in their thirties who have never known someone who has died, but in the first century, this would have been impossible.

There is a story told of the Buddha about a woman who could not leave the graveyard, for she could not bear to leave behind the corpse of her baby. When she encountered the Buddha, she begged him for medicine that would restore her child to life. The Buddha felt compassion for her and promised her that if she could bring back some mustard from a house that had not known death, he would give her such medicine. Mustard was a common spice, and every house had some, but as she went from door to door, she discovered that every single house had had someone die within its walls. She returned to the Buddha empty-handed, but changed. Her child's death was put in perspective for her and she was able to leave her child behind. She grasped the truth of impermanence, and followed the Buddha from that moment on.

Life in ancient Israel was no different. Death was everywhere. Many religions promised a way to cheat death, or to ultimately escape it. Greek thought held that while the body was ephemeral, the soul was immortal, and continued to live on after the death of the body. Pharaisaical Judaism speculated a resurrection of the body, for the Jews could not bear the notion of a disembodied existence divorced from sensual pleasure. Later Christianity tried to have it both ways, acknowledging both the immortality of the soul, but also the eventual reunion of the soul with a glorified body similar to the one Jesus was believed to have had after the resurrection.

Death can come at any time

Most religions, however they imagined life after death, agree that the decisions that a person makes before death impact the quality of the afterlife. The Jesus of Thomas shares this opinion, for he says, "Look to the living one while you are living, lest you die and then seek to see him, and find that you cannot" (59).

There is an urgency about this warning: time is running out! If we are to find an answer to death, we must find it before we die, and as time is marching on mercilessly, we have a narrowing window of time in which to act. Jesus illustrates this dramatically in the following story:

> There was a man of great wealth who possessed many riches. He said, 'I will make use of my riches, so that I might sow and reap and plant and fill my storehouse with fruit, so that I will never lack for anything." These were the thoughts he entertained about his riches, and yet that same night, he died. He who has ears should listen! (63)

This verse, which has parallels in the canonical gospels, warns that neither wealth nor good planning can safeguard one against the

Reaper. Death often comes as a surprise, or as a thief in the night as described in Verse 21:

> Mary said to Jesus, "What do your disciples resemble?"
>
> He answered her, "They resemble small children dwelling in a field which does not belong to them. When the owners of the field come, they will say, "Give our field back to us." They will strip naked before them, in order to give everything back, and to return their field.
>
> Therefore I say, if the head of the household knows that the burgler is coming , he will keep watch beforehand and will not allow him to sneak into his house – his kingdom – to steal his possessions. You, however, should all keep watch from the beginning of the world, bind to yourselves great power, so that no thieves will fall upon you on the road, because the help which you look for will fall upon you.
>
> Let there be in your midst a person who understands. When the fruit split open, he came in a hurry, his sickle in his hand, and he reaped. The one who has ears to hear should listen!

This odd assemblage of images is just barely coherent, but as a cluster of warnings about the immediacy of death it is pertinent to our discussion. Jesus says his disciples are like children dwelling in a field that does not belong to them. This is the world itself, and when the owners come and demand their field back, the disciples will strip naked and return everything.

This is what death does to us. This world is not ours, we are squatters living on both borrowed land and time. We come into the world naked, and we leave it the same way. We take nothing with us except our soul, which has either atrophied or grown depending on how we have tended it during our lives. If we are not careful, if we have not grown our soul, it will be taken from us, and we will surely die. But if we are cautious we will give our soul attention by "binding to ourselves great power" so that it cannot be stolen.

Once again, mindfulness plays an important role here. "You, however, should all keep watch from the beginning of the world," Jesus says. This is reminiscent of the Buddha, who said, "Like a border town that is well guarded both within and without, so let a man guard himself, and let not a moment pass by in carelessness. Those who carelessly allow their life to pass by, in the end have to suffer in hell" (Dhammapada, 22:315).

Jesus is clear that there is much at stake here: if one does not find the secret to immortality before one dies, then one's fate is simply worm-food. We are to be mindful and cautious, not distracted by wealth or sensual pleasures or our own despair. There is a way, Jesus promises, to escape death, by finding "a place of peace," and "binding to yourselves great power." But what does he mean by this, and how is it to be achieved?

What causes death?

Escaping death involves understanding its cause. Paul, in his version of Christianity, asserted a causal link between sin and death. In his epistle to the Romans he wrote, "The wages of sin is death (6:23)," and linked the fact that all human beings die to the sin of Adam (1 Cor. 15:22). Such theologizing is the origin of many bizarre ideas in the history of Christianity, such as "original sin" which, according to Augustine, is transmitted through semen. But for most Jews of Jesus' time, sin was not seen in such a spiritualized way.

The Law of Moses was seen as a practical set of rules that safeguarded the community that kept it in a very immediate way. People did not avoid sin because of some persistent curse on the species, but because there were real and obvious benefits for doing so. Adultery caused dangerous strife in a small community, pork and shellfish could indeed be dangerous menu items in a desert. People avoided sin not only for abstract theological reasons, but simply so that they would survive.

Curiously, the Gospel of Thomas sidesteps the notion of sin entirely, effectively denying the link between sin and death. *Sin is simply not the problem.* The causal agent for death is not sin, but ignorance: buying into the illusion of separateness. Thomas denies any difference between sin and righteousness, the notion that they are different things is a mistake. Instead, he redefines righteousness as the ability to see without any distinctions.

In this he echoes the philosophy of the Taoist sage Chuang Tzu, who wrote,

> Life, death, preservations, loss, failure, success, poverty, riches, worthiness, unworthiness, slander, fame, hunger, thirst, cold, heat, these are the alternations of the world.... Day and night they change place before us and wisdom cannot spy out their source. Therefore, they should not be enough to destroy your harmony. The Way has never known any boundaries.... So, those who divide fail to divide; those who discriminate fail to discriminate. What does this mean, you ask? The sage embraces things. Ordinary men discriminate among them and parade their discriminations before others. So I say, those who discriminate fail to see (73).

The righteous person is one who lives in harmony with all things, who sees their essential oneness, who eschews distinction as illusion and folly. The holy person lives "welcoming to all," in Mechtild's words (126), and can embrace all things. One who does not see the oneness of all things is trapped in ignorance, and therefore subject to the ravages of death.

Jesus said, "Adam came to be out of a great power and great wealth, and yet he did not become worthy of you. For if he was worthy he would not have tasted death" (85). Worthiness, in Thomas' system, is not based on power, or wealth, or righteousness as it was conventionally understood, but upon insight, unitive consciousness – in other words, *knowledge*.

Just as there is a relationship between ignorance and death, one causing the other, there is a similar relationship between knowledge and eternal life. But how does knowledge of Oneness deliver a person from death?

The antidote to death

So long as our identity is invested in our ego, or in the notion that who we are is this limited, finite self, then we are lost. If we are this body, then when this body dies, we die. If, however, we take the teachings of the Jesus of Thomas to heart, if we can not only understand the essential oneness of all things, but through practice and successive revelation, actually internalize this truth so that it *becomes* truth and not simply a novel idea, then an amazing thing happens to us. Our identity shifts from this bag of bones (and the chatterbox ego that inhabits it) to the universe itself. We become the universe, and the universe becomes us. *And the universe lives forever.* If by the time of our death we have succeeded in transferring our identity from the ego to the universe, we too will live forever. The body may die, but we do not die, because we are not the body. We are the All, which is eternal.

This is the shift that the Jesus of Thomas asks us to make: a shift in identity. Sin is not the problem – the illusion that we are separate beings with limited life spans is the problem. If we can break the power this illusion holds over us, then we break through to immortality. For Thomas Christians, this shift *is* salvation, and is the goal of all spiritual practice.

Jesus said, "When you bring forth that which is within you, that which you bring forth will save you. If you do not bring forth what is in you, that which you fail to bring forth will condemn you" (70). Our true self is not the ego, but the All. If we can bring forth this true identity and claim it for our own, this will be our salvation.

But if we fail to acknowledge our true self, then we are condemned to die. This is not a judgment from any outside God or jury. It is simply the way it is. If you identify with your body and your mind, you will die when they die. If you identify with the All, then you are eternal. The choice is yours.

As we have seen in previous chapters, achieving unitive consciousness – identity with the All – is a kind of rebirth. We are simply not the same being before this shift in perception that we are after. Meister Eckhart echoes Jesus' words when he promises that, "In this birth you will discover all blessing. But neglect this birth and you neglect all blessing. Tend only to this birth in you and you will find there all goodness and all consolation, all delight, all being and all truth" (76).

For human beings, there is no greater enemy than death. From the moment we realize that we will die, the spectre of death hovers over our shoulders to remind us that our time is coming, and soon. Our religious practices reinforce this sense of terror and ephemerality: Buddhists practice dying daily, yoga practitioners end each session in a "death pose," and Christian priests smear ashes on the foreheads of believers, reminding them that "they are dust, and to dust" they shall return. Yet death is, for the Jesus of Thomas, just another false distinction. There is only the One, eternally in flux, transforming from one shape to another. Once we identify with this One, death has no more power over us.

Lao Tzu, in the Tao Te Ching, speaks to this truth eloquently:

> If you can empty yourself of everything,
> you will have lasting peace.
> Things arise, but I contemplate their return.
> Things flourish and grow, and then return to their Source.
> To return to the Source is to know perfect peace.
> I call this a return to Life.
>
> Returning to Life is a Universal Constant.
> Knowing this is illuminating.
> Someone who doesn't understand this is in error
> and may act dangerously.
> But knowing this Constant, you can embrace all things.
> Embracing all things, you can treat them fairly.
> Treating them fairly, you are noble.
> Being noble, you are like the cosmos.
> If you are like the cosmos, you are like the Tao.
>
> If you are like the Tao, you will have eternal life,
> and you needn't be afraid of dying. (16)

Spiritual exercises

1. **Practice transferring your identity from your ego to the All.** This is, of course, not nearly as easy as it sounds, and requires all the efforts, disciplines, and learnings we have covered so far. Transferring your identity is a goal to work towards, not something you can simply **do**, like tying your shoe or buying a soda. During your daily meditation practice, contemplate the saying of Jesus, "I am the All, from me all things have emerged and to me all things have been revealed." Use it as an affirmation, not as the words of Jesus, but indeed as your own words. You may want to use them as a mantra. Work with these words until they are true for you, until there is a deep inner sense of their rightness.

2. **Practice dying.** In your imagination, practice seeing yourself not as your body, but as the universe. From this perspective, watch your own body fail, fall, and die. Watch the flesh disintegrate into dust, become earth, and nourish a tender green shoot. Watch how life perpetuates itself, how death and birth are inextricably linked, and how you-as-the-universe both transcend and participate in this process. Repeat this visualization until you feel comfortable letting go of your body, and joy at the cycle of transformation that is your true life.

Religion is the problem, not the solution

Every action of God is new, for he makes all things new.
God is the newest thing there is; the youngest thing there is.
God is the beginning and if we are united
to him we become new again.

– Meister Eckhart (32)

These days many people make a distinction between "being spiritual" and "being religious." Being spiritual is generally seen as a good thing: spiritual people are sensitive to the movements of their own souls, kind to themselves and others, and are respectful of the diverse ways in which other people express their own spiritualities. Being religious, however, carries quite a different set of assumptions, most of them not so good: religious people are often viewed as being dogmatic, obsessive, and intolerant of beliefs that diverge from their own, even in minute ways.

While these stereotypes are far from accurate – there are plenty of unkind people who see themselves as spiritual, and lots of tolerant religious folk – they are, nevertheless, widespread. And admitting that such characterizations are oversimplifications, we should also be able to see that there is a grain of truth in them. Even as we raise our hand to object, there is a part of us that is saying, "yes, that's right" at the very same time.

Jesus in Thomas embodies this very ambivalence. Though he does not use the word "spirituality" or "religion" his teaching very clearly makes a distinction between an honest engagement with the Divine and blind obedience to tradition. Yet he does not reject tradition out of hand, only the uncritical practice of it, which divorces the means from the end. Once, when Jesus and his disciples were spending a quiet Sabbath afternoon wandering in a wheat field, some of them rolled some wheat and popped the kernels into their mouths. Some "religious folk" saw this and were outraged – rolling wheat is work, which was forbidden on the Sabbath! Yet Jesus counters them by saying, "The Sabbath was made for man, not man for the Sabbath" (Mark 2:27). Religion is supposed to provide for basic human needs: comfort, meaning, hope. Yet too often, those who practice religious traditions forget the purpose of it all, and raise up the tradition itself as an idol.

This is as true in our day as in Jesus' own. The Roman Catholic sexual abuse scandals have painfully revealed where the hierarchy's true concern lies: not with the victims of the abuse, but in protecting and maintaining the institution. Likewise, fundamentalist evangelicals routinely reject and shun their own family members for being gay or lesbian. This sort of behavior is not limited to Christians, of course. Fundamentalist Muslims have waged a campaign of terror against the West, killing innocent people in the name of the mercy and justice of God, while fundamentalist Jews are complicit with the terror in Israel because of their own stubbornness and lack of empathy towards the Palestinians.

It is this very irony at the heart of religious observance that makes Jesus' critique of the religion of his day so relevant for us now. Little has changed, apparently, except for our capacity for rapid bloodshed, and the immediacy of our witnessing of it all over the world. More ironic still is that it is the religious leaders – those who are versed in scripture and tradition, and by all accounts should know better – that are the worst offenders, because it is they who educate the masses in ignorance and incite the violence that is so abhorrent to any sensitive, truly spiritual soul. Jesus said in Matthew's Gospel that it would be better to tie a millstone around one's neck and jump into the ocean than to lead one of God's innocents astray (18:6). "Astray" is usually understood to mean deviating from the accepted religious orthodoxy, but Jesus means instead a deviation from the true will of the Spirit.

This is an important distinction in the Gospel of Thomas, as well. Once, when Jesus was preaching, many people became indignant at his words. His own disciples confronted him, saying, "Who do you think you are, saying such things to us?" Jesus answers, "You do not realize who I am from the things I say. Rather you are like those Jews who either love the tree and hate its fruit, or love the fruit and hate the tree" (43).

The tree in this verse is the Jewish tradition, which is intended to bring forth the fruit of true spirituality. But just as in our own day, there were those back then who obsessively embraced religious tradition to the exclusion of real communion with Divinity. Likewise, there were those who love the fruit (spirituality) but hate the tree (religion), just like those today who say they are "spiritual but not religious." But Jesus rejects both extremes, affirming the usefulness of tradition, but not confusing it with the true goal.

Religious extremists were in no short supply in Jesus' day. The Sadducees sprung from the priestly tribe, and they administered the operation of the Temple, where the sacrificial rituals were performed according to the Law of Moses. The Sadducees taught that, so long as the proper rituals were enacted, all would be well between Israel and its God. They did not waste time with metaphysical speculation and rejected the notion of an afterlife, believing that God's faithfulness to them primarily took the form of their survival as a people. They were politically pragmatic, cooperating with their Roman occupiers so long as Rome allowed them to stay in power. This was not entirely selfish, but in fact, it was also spiritually motivated. So long as Rome allowed them to continue their position of power, the appointed sacrifices could continue, and God's favor towards Israel could be assured.

In opposition to the Sadducees were the Pharisees, who, though respecting and adhering to the sacrificial requirements of the temple, also emphasized personal piety as the way to a proper relationship with the Divine. For them, it was not enough to simply offer the appropriate sacrifices once per year – true intimacy with Divinity meant making one's life a sacrifice. One must take to heart the requirements of the Mosaic Law, "bind them upon one's forehead and forearm," (Deut. 6:8) knowing and keeping over 600 requirements. The intent of such rigorous practice was to remind oneself of the divine presence at all times, and of one's proper relationship to it – never a bad goal. Yet, too often, this goal (which is indeed a valuable form of spirituality) was obscured by the means, a system of religious requirements that became increasingly obsessive and legalistic. People became more concerned with what other people thought of them – the appearance of holiness – than in their actual spiritual state. It was to these Pharisees that Jesus said, in verse 89, "For what reason do you wash the outside of a cup? Don't you understand that whoever created the inside is the same one who made the outside?" The cup is like a person: why bother making sure the outside appears clean if the inside is filthy?

The Sadducees and Pharisees represent the two main streams of Jewish spiritual thought in Jesus' day, but there were also the fringe groups. Isolationists like the Essenes believed that the rote observance of the Sadducees was spiritually dead, that in effect, the priesthood was vacant or, worse, apostate. So they separated themselves from mainstream Jewish life, trying to capture a "pure" form of devotion in the Judaean desert that would be pleasing to God.

There were also the Zealots, who believed that any form of foreign domination was unacceptable, and wanted to overthrow the yoke of Rome at any cost. They pointed to the biblical record of the miraculous victories of the Jewish armies in their history. Time and again, God assisted them in their battles, granting them victory even when they were hopelessly outnumbered. The Zealots had faith that God would deliver them again, if the nation would only trust enough to rise and take up their arms.

Of all of these groups, Jesus had the most affinity with the

Pharisees, and as noted previously, it was this tradition out of which he came and in which he taught. The leaders of the Pharisees were called rabbis, "teachers," and indeed, Jesus was a rabbi in this tradition. Like other Pharisees, Jesus believed that constant awareness of the divine Presence was a primary spiritual goal, but he frequently disagreed with the methods of his co-religionists, which were as likely to distract from their goal as to assist the seeker in reaching it.

Jesus reserved his most pointed critiques for his own philosophical school, the Pharisees. And criticize he did. In verse 34, Jesus said, "If a blind person leads a blind person, they both fall into a ditch." Someone who has forsaken true spirituality for religion is spiritually blind, and anyone who follows in such a way dooms him- or herself to like blindness. Of course such criticism is not applicable only to Pharisees, but anyone for whom religion has eclipsed spirituality. Jesus' words are echoed by the Buddha, when he said of his own religious leaders, the Brahmins,

> When these Brahmins teach a path that they do not know or see, saying, "This is the only straight path," this cannot possibly be right. Just as a file of blind men go on, clinging to each other, and the first one sees nothing, the middle one sees nothing, and the last one sees nothing – so it is with the talk of these Brahmins (Digha Nikaya 13:15).

Hypocrisy

One of the things that upset Jesus most was the hypocrisy of his fellow Pharisees. Their rabbis were not only concerned with keeping the many required rules – and making sure others saw and respected their piety, but they were also concerned that others followed suit. Again, this was not an entirely selfish enterprise, for they believed that their survival as a people depended upon God's good favor, which was to be won not (as the Sadducees supposed) by keeping the requirements of the temple code, but by the genuine piety of the Jewish people as a whole.

The result was that some people were very zealous in making sure that others cultivated an appropriately pious life, and kept all the rules, even as they did. But the Jesus of Thomas does not see salvation in terms of the physical survival of Israel, but as conscious union with Divinity. Thus, he had little patience for the "moral policeman" posture some of the Pharisees struck. To them, he says, "You see the speck in your brother's eye, but you do not see the log in your own eye. When you remove the log from your own eye, then you will be able to see well enough to remove the speck from your brother's eye" (26). This is a cutting critique, for the size of the offense of those who do not – or cannot – live up to the strict moral code of the Pharisees is likened by Jesus to a "speck" while the supplanting of real spirituality by fundamentalist legalism warrants a "log" in his estimation.

Once again, there is an echo of the Buddha in Jesus' words, for, addressing a similar situation, the Awakened One said, "If a man sees the sins of others and forever thinks of their faults, his own sins increase forever and far off is he from the end of his faults" (Dhammapada, 18:253).

But the tragedy of such hypocrisy is not simply the fact that the hypocrite alone is denying him- or herself a genuine spiritual life, but that, when such a person is in a position of spiritual authority, he or she prevents others from enjoying a truly spiritual life as well. Jesus pulls no punches when he warns, "Woe to the Pharisees, for they are like a dog resting on the oxen's manger – it neither eats, nor allows the oxen to eat" (102).

This image, in which the "hay" of true spiritual communion is a commodity to be guarded, even hoarded, presages the attitude of the Pauline Christians who would follow later in Jesus' name, hoarding the "grace" of the sacraments, and doling them out only to those they deemed "acceptable." Likewise, the "keys of the kingdom" held by the Christian church are evoked by the following saying: "The Pharisees and the scribes took the Keys of Knowledge and hid them; they neither entered nor allowed anyone who wanted to go in to enter. You, however, be cunning as serpents, and innocent as doves" (39).

This is not to impugn the Pharisees or the Christians who follow them, among whom were many sensitive and spiritual souls, but only to reveal the folly and hypocrisy of valuing religion over immediate spiritual experience. For a spiritual leader to do so is to hide the Keys of Knowledge, to sit on the hay of spiritual nourishment, to thus separate the common people from the spiritual treasure that is the proper inheritance of all peoples, indeed all beings.

Huang Po, a mystic of the Ch'an school of Buddhism, had similarly terse words for the spiritual leaders of his own day. He told his community, "You are all like drunks – if you go about busying yourselves in this way, when will you notice the present moment? Don't you know there are no teachers of Ch'an in all the land?" One monk raised his hand and said, "But what about those who lead spiritual communities?" Huang Po answered him, "I did not say there is no Ch'an, just that there are no teachers" (*Blue Cliff Record*, 72).

Huang Po, like Jesus, does not deny that people are having genuine encounters with the Holy, only that those who have set themselves up as leaders are often more of a hindrance than a help in this regard. Their hypocrisy frustrates the genuine impulse toward the Divine inherent in all beings, and through their misguided teaching they unwittingly doom the trusting souls that follow their instruction.

Jesus, in the interest of true spirituality, comes to destroy religion as it is commonly understood. He says as much in verse 71: "I will destroy this house, and no one will ever build it again." While later Christians would understand "this house" to refer to his own body (which they believed to be crucified and resurrected in a new form), most scholars believe that he was actually referring to the Temple. The Temple was metonymous for the entire sacrificial ritual system the Judaism of the time was built upon. Though the temple would indeed be destroyed by the Romans forty years after Jesus' ministry, his words were less a prophesy in the sense of foretelling the future as they were prophetic, simply telling the truth: true spirituality cannot be forever thwarted, and when religion stands in its way, that religion must of necessity fall.

Later Jewish Christians would not have appreciated the distinction, and saw the destruction of the Temple as God's just judgement upon a corrupt religious system. Nonetheless, their poetry reveals their sensitivity to this conflict between spirituality and religion. In the beautiful Odes of Solomon, they wrote:

> A stream erupts into a wide and endless river
> That floods and, breaking, carries away the temple.
> Ordinary men, and even those whose art is to stem
> Rough waters, cannot hold it back,
> And the river covers the face of the whole earth.
> The river fills everything,
> And the thirsty of the earth drink and satisfy thirst.
> The drink comes from the highest one.

> *(Song 6, Barnstone/Meyer 361.)*

In this poem, the water of true spirituality wells up and carries away the temple, the symbol of rote religion. No man can stem its torrent, and the thirst of every soul is quenched.

Jesus seems to contradict his own unitive vision when he characterizes such mindless observance as being "outside" of God in verse 40: "A grapevine has been planted outside the Father, and, cut off from its nourishment, it will be pulled up by its root and destroyed." Since all things are in God (indeed, all things *are* God) this is a statement typical of Jesus' fondness for hyperbole, or overstatement. There is nothing "outside the Father" yet legalistic approaches to religion certainly fall outside of what God intends or, in Jesus' opinion, approves of. Such religion is cut off from its "nourishment," from the unstoppable torrent of living water, and will be "pulled up by its root and destroyed." When the Jewish Christians saw the destruction of the Temple, they could not help but remember these words, and must have felt they were witnessing God's judgment first-hand.

The ineffectiveness of spiritual disciplines

The proponents of legalistic religion were obsessed with "doing the right thing," and equated the keeping of all the proscribed laws with holiness and righteousness. But it was not only important to be observant, but to be seen by others to be so. For the very religious, one's social standing in the community of "holy" people depended largely upon how perfectly one was perceived to abide by these laws. Jesus' critique was often that such people were more concerned with how holy they appeared to others than with how genuinely connected to Spirit they were.

"Doing the right thing" was much harder than it sounded. Ancient Israel had developed a complex system of spiritual disciplines intended to advance one's holiness. Such practices as prayer, fasting, almsgiving, and abstaining from certain foods, were – and still are – important practices in nearly every religious tradition. It is natural that, having been reared in a legalistic system, Jesus' followers would also be concerned with "doing the right thing" and would look to him to define that for them.

In verses 6 and 14, Jesus confronts these questions directly. His disciples questioned him, saying, "Do you want us to fast? And how should we pray? Should we give alms? And what foods should we abstain from?" Jesus said to them, "If you fast, you will bring forth sin, and if you pray, others will condemn you, and if you give alms, you will create evil in your souls."

This must have shocked his hearers, for whom such practices had always been synonymous with righteous living. But for Jesus, such practices divorced from the true spirituality they were intended to evoke were simply dishonest. "Do not tell lies," he told them, referring directly to such practices, "and do not do what you hate, for all things are disclosed to heaven." God is not fooled by pious observance – God knows the heart, and knows the true motivations for one's spiritual observances. As Meister Eckhart put it five hundred years ago, "It is when people are not aware of God's presence everywhere that they must seek God by special methods and special practices. Such people have not attained God. To all outward appearances persons who continue properly in their pious practices are holy. Inwardly, however, they are asses. For they know about God, but do not know God" (59).

Jesus goes even further, directly contradicting his fellow rabbis. To those who have always been told to be extremely scrupulous in keeping kosher (the dietary restrictions of Jewish law), Jesus said, "If you go into any land, and walk the territories, eat whatever people put in front of you." Hospitality, apparently, goes both ways. And since, in the theology of Thomas, all distinctions are illusory, the notion of "proper" or "improper" foods is simply meaningless, especially when such observance limits one's ability to be welcoming to those who welcome you. Jesus' words at the end of verse 14 are a stinging rebuke to proponents of legalist religion in any age: "It is not what goes into your mouth that will defile you. Rather, it is what comes out of your mouth that will defile you."

This was a radical teaching in his day. It echoes the Buddha, who told his own followers: "Stealing, deceiving, adultery; this is defilement. Not the eating of meat" (Sutta Nipata 242). Jesus and the Buddha are clear: laws and restrictions may indeed form the warp and woof of religion, but they cannot in themselves affect the state of the soul. An enlightened person may choose to eat or not eat certain things, but culinary selection will not confer enlightenment.

Even more dangerously, the Jesus of Thomas scorned circumcision, a practice the Jews had long held dear to distinguish them from their gentile neighbors. The practice goes all the way back to the time of Moses. In a surprising and inexplicable episode in the book of Exodus (4:25) God is roaring through the camp where Moses and his family are living, hoping to find and kill Moses. Moses' wife, Zipporah, hoping to appease God's bloodlust, cuts the foreskin from her baby's penis and offers it to God in place of Moses' own life.

This episode is a foreshadowing of the Jews' slaughtering a lamb and painting the lintels of their houses with it so that the Angel of Death would pass over their houses untouched, while entering the houses of the Egyptians to kill the first born sons and animals. After the Jews gained their freedom, circumcision was proclaimed law – all male children must be so cut as a sign of the covenant between God and the people.

Yet when the disciples ask Jesus about this ancient and revered practice in verse 104, Jesus' answers them, "If it were a good thing, fathers would beget sons from their mothers already circumcised. The true circumcision of the spirit, however, is utterly profitable." Once again Jesus makes a distinction between the outward show of religion and the inward reality of true communion with the One. To cut away a person's foreskin indicates participation in a community, but has nothing to do with whether a person has achieved unitive consciousness. Circumcision of the Spirit, however, cuts away the ego – a truly needless thing in Thomas' system – and is not simply a sign of a covenant, but is itself true communion. Circumcision of the flesh may be, in the Buddha's words, the finger pointing at the moon, but circumcision of the spirit is the moon itself.

We don't know if Jesus' opinions about the generally accepted spiritual disciplines of his day were truly as strong as Thomas indicates, or whether, as I mentioned earlier, they are examples of Jesus' penchant for hyperbole. Yet over and over again in the Gospel of Thomas, Jesus drives home a single point: One is not made holy by refusing to eat certain foods, or restricting one's activities in myriad ways. One is only made holy by transcending categories such as sinner/saint, clean/unclean, proper/improper, etc. There are no clean things and no unclean things. In fact, there are no things. There is only the One, and beyond that we are simply fooling ourselves.

Holiness means "wholeness," not "purity." Holiness only comes to us when we are able to embrace the universe as a whole, complete with all its shadow and light. When Jesus told his disciples, "Be ye perfect, as your father in heaven is perfect," (Matt. 5:48) the word for "perfect" is a mistranslation. A better rendering is "complete," or "whole." To be "complete" as God is complete means to be whole, to embrace oneself with all of one's parts, and to embrace the world in the same way.

Holiness is not about what you shut out – it's about what you let in. To embrace the whole world, indeed the whole universe, as oneself is truly the fruit of unitive knowing. Mechtild of Magdeburg instructs us to, "Live welcoming to all." This is a hospitality that transcends manners and food regulations – it is a hospitality that makes room for everyone and everything at one's table, without qualifications or distinctions. It is a gracious "yes" to all of life.

You say you want a revolution

Saying "yes" to all of life was a dangerous thing in Jesus' day. Israel was filled with zealots at the time – those who wanted to overthrow Rome by force. These were people desperate for a revolution. Yet the kind of revolution Jesus intended was far more radical than what they envisioned, for it called not for the overthrow of the government, but the overthrow of the ego.

Besides proper and improper foods and actions, there were definitely proper and improper people with whom one could and could not associate. In Jesus' time a religiously observant Jew would not mix socially with a gentile (non-Jewish person), certainly not with a Roman, since they were the enemy, the occupiers. One could not even associate with Samaritans, who were partly of Jewish lineage, but worshipped differently than the Jews in Israel. Even amongst Jews there were many people whom it was not proper to be seen with. The list is not much different today: prostitutes, traitors, and thieves. Although today we may substitute "lawyers" for "tax collectors," the sentiment was similar.

Yet when Jesus began preaching his message of unitive consciousness, he found the religious people were simply not interested. They already had everything figured out, and no wet-behind-the-ears rabbi from the red-light district of Galilee was going to tell them any different. So instead, he took his message to those whom the religious elite had rejected: those very same prostitutes, traitors, and tax collectors so anathema in "appropriate" society.

In verse 64 he relates a parable illustrating this very situation:

> Jesus said, "A man was hosting some visitors, and when he had prepared a feast he sent his servant to call the visitors.

He went to the first and said to him, 'My Lord calls for
you.' He answered, 'I have some money intended for some
merchants; they are meeting me tonight, and I must go and
place my order. I beg to be excused from the dinner.'

So he went to another of the visitors. He said to them, 'My
Lord has called for you.' He answered him, 'I have bought a
house, and am required all day – no rest for me!'

So he went to another one, and said to him, 'My Lord
calls you.' He answered him, 'My friend is getting married,
and I have to prepare the dinner. I can't come, and ask to be
excused from the feast.'

He went to another, and said to him, 'My Lord calls for
you.' But he said, 'I have bought a farm, and must go collect
the rent. I can't come, and hope to be excused.'

The servant went back to his Lord and said, 'All those you
invited to your feast have begged off.'

The Lord said to his servant, 'Go outside, to the streets,
and whomever you meet, bring them in to dine. The buyers
and the traders may not enter the places of my father."

In this story, all the "proper" people are invited to the feast first, but
when none of them come, the doors are thrown open to whoever
would come. Likewise, those who know the religion already have
their invitations, and have declined to join the feast. They have
everything they need to point them to knowledge of the One, yet
persist in missing the point, settling for religion rather than the
true spirituality it is supposed to facilitate.

This practice of associating with all the "wrong" sorts of folks
caused Jesus no small amount of conflict, as the gospels are
filled with stories of angry Pharisees confronting Jesus about the
company he keeps (see Matt. 9, Mark 2, Luke 5). Yet the Jesus of
Thomas is not "the Prince of Peace," as depicted elsewhere. Instead,
Jesus says bluntly, "Perhaps people are thinking that I have come
to cast peace upon the world. What they do not know is that I have
come to cast division upon the earth – fire, sword, war. For there
will be five people in a house, and three of them will be against the

other two, and two against the three; the father will be against the son, and the son against the father; and they will stand to their feet, alone."

Contradicting the prevailing religious notions of his day won Jesus few fans amongst those who put great store by their own righteousness, and he had no illusions that it would be any different for those who followed his teachings. He knew that his teachings would set those followers who came from conservative religious homes against their own parents and siblings. He knew that anyone who walked in his way would not be welcome in the synagogues or the temple. But there was no way to soft-sell his message, no way to temper it to make it more palatable to the "proper" people. In a society that defined itself by who and what is proper and who and what is not, no one proclaiming that such lines of demarcation are unimportant – or worse, illusory – would get a favorable hearing.

Jesus was no idiot – he knew his teaching would bring nothing but trouble. Yet he was prepared to face the consequences, and tried to prepare his listeners, as well. In verse ten, Jesus tells them, "I have cast fire upon the world, and see, I am tending it until it burns." This is not simply the fire of animosity or strife, but the fire of truth. The teaching of Jesus burns away all that is illusory and impedes true communion with divinity: the ego, distinctions and demarcations, even religion itself, all is consumed in the fire of consciousness until only the One remains. Note that Jesus is tending the blaze until the world itself burns. Once one has surrendered to unitive consciousness, there is no place on earth that illusion may find safe quarter. All such chaff and dross are consumed in this flame.

Mechtild in her poetry uses less violent imagery, yet promises the same result: "God says, 'When your Easter comes, I shall be all around you, I shall be through and through you, and I shall steal your body and give you to your Love'" (95). When our "Easter" comes – when we finally succeed in shifting our identity from our ego and body to the One that is the universe – our body will be stolen and Love will be given us in its place. We will know absolutely that our body is not who we truly are, and the things that pertain to the body, including religion itself, will be likewise robbed of import. Only Love, the One, will remain. And we are that One.

True spirituality

With all of this pointed, often heated, critique of religion, it would be easy to mistake Jesus for someone who "hates the tree" of religion but "loves the fruit" of spirituality. Yet it is important to bear in mind that criticism is not the same as antipathy. Just as we in the United States are adamant that loving our country includes criticizing how it is run, loving our religious traditions must by necessity involve a critical evaluation of them.

In Matthew's Gospel, Jesus says, "I come not to abolish the law, but to fulfill it" (5:17). Jesus is not interested in doing away with Judaism, but with loving it enough to correct its course. This is an overwhelming task, and Jesus did not succeed in reforming his religion. But as U2 sing, "I cannot change the world, but I can change the world in me," so Jesus, while not altering the trajectory of Pharisaic Judaism, nonetheless changed the spiritual lives of everyone he touched.

So what does a healthy relationship between religion and spirituality look like? How can they work toward the same goal, instead of being in conflict?

Let us return to that marvelous verse, 22, where Jesus says, "When you make an eye in the place of an eye and a hand in the place of a hand, and a foot in the place of a foot, and an image in the place of an image, then you will enter the Kingdom." One way to understand this verse is that a person cannot use a religion off-the-shelf, but must fashion one from scratch. I grew up in a very conservative religious home, went to church every time the door was open, and even surrendered to preach at the age of sixteen. But I did not meet Jesus in the church of my birth, in fact I did not have a truly life-changing encounter with him until I went to the Episcopal church in college. It was there that I learned that faith was more than a list of do's and don'ts, and began walking a path of true communion with Divinity. I could not use a religion simply handed to me by my parents; I had to fashion one from the raw materials of scripture, tradition, reason, and my own lived experience. I had to make "an eye in place of an eye" for the one given to me did not see clearly. I had to fashion "a foot in place of a foot," because the legalistic faith of my childhood could not get me where I needed to go. I had to conjure "an image in place of an image," because the image of God offered by the fundamentalist faith was sorely flawed.

The mistake most people make in evaluating religious traditions is they assume everything a tradition says must be taken at face value, or as interpreted by the school with which they are most familiar. Since the surface interpretation, or the fundamentalist interpretation being offered is clearly unacceptable to most people, they simply dismiss the entire tradition as being pointless or false. This is tragic since most religious traditions have a wealth of beauty, truth, and insight to offer. And all religious traditions experience a struggle between their conservative and liberal poles, between literalism and interpretation, between religion and spirituality.

The goal is to find the proper balance – a religious tradition without the fruit of spirituality is pointless, but spirituality without the tree of religious tradition is rootless and ungrounded. Since religion often has a stranglehold on spirituality, we must find a way to hold religion more lightly, and to give spirituality its proper esteem. Meister Eckhart gives us a clue as to how to do this. He wrote, "I pray God to rid me of God. The highest and loftiest thing that one can let go of is to let go of God for the sake of God" (50).

The image of God we are given as children is often woefully inadequate. We must allow that God to die so that we can establish a meaningful relationship with a God of our mature understanding. We must fashion "an image in place of an image," in order to enter the Kingdom. For those of us who hold Thomas in high esteem, we must let go of the notion of God as the old man in the sky searching out sinners to throw thunderbolts at, for if we do not, we cannot truly embrace the God who is simply All That Is.

But once we make this shift – once we give ourselves permission to fire the god of our childhood and enter into true communion with the One – suddenly the symbols, stories, and rituals of our traditions are transformed, and become infused with new and transcendent meaning that was invisible to us before. Our traditions can often take us by surprise by becoming suddenly relevant again!

Jesus speaks of this very phenomenon when he said, "Images are revealed to people, and the light within them is hidden in the image of the light of the father. He will be revealed and his image hidden by his light." Trapped in our former understanding of our religion, a concept of God was presented to us ("images are revealed to people"), but the true light of God is obscured by the faulty image (it is hard to truly trust and love an angry and vengeful god). Yet by fashioning "an image in place of an image" and embracing a new understanding of divinity, God "will be revealed" and every image or concept we could possibly hold of God is obscured by the light of truth.

With this new orientation, religion is remade, and is now in the service of true spirituality, grounding it in history and in the lived experience of those who have gone before. Images are interpreted to wrest from them their value rather than set up on pedestals as idols to be worshipped.

Spirituality as social suicide

Making such a shift can be, in some communities, severely frowned upon. In conservative religious traditions, new interpretations are not often welcome, and many a person who has experienced a life-changing epiphany has also experienced the cold-shoulder from the "faithful." Merely changing your own orientation can imply a critique of how others are living out their spiritual lives, and when those others are in positions of authority, trouble is rarely far behind. Jesus discovered this in his own ministry, and experienced many close calls. In Luke's Gospel, he was worshipping in a synagogue in his home town of Nazareth. He was asked to read the appointed text, and afterwards revealed his insight that the prophesy recorded in Isaiah was speaking about him (4:16-19). Of course, it is the occupation of any exegete worth his or her salt to make ancient passages relevant to themselves and their hearers, but this is not how Jesus' fellow worshippers interpreted his statement. Before Jesus could turn around he was attacked and had to run for his life.

It may have been occasions such as this that prompted him to remark to his followers, "No prophet is accepted in his own village; no physician heals those who know him" (31). Though no doubt speaking about his own experience, Jesus' statement also clearly speaks to us as well. Many of us have had the painful experience of going through a life-changing spiritual awakening, only to have our insights mocked and derided by those who are supposed to love us. While we may feel "born again" and engaged with a vibrant spirituality, we usually seem like the same hopeless shlubs to our family members. Or worse, they may feel threatened by the implied critiques provided by the new insights. In extreme cases, which unfortunately are not rare, people are shunned, declared dead to their relatives because of their "heresy."

But know it or not, all heretics are in good company. Every religious leader that has ever impacted the spiritual life of humankind has started his or her career out as a heretic. Just look at the Buddha, Lao Tzu, Martin Luther, the Beguines, or, more contemporaneously, Rosa Parks. All of them are heretics, dissenting from the prevailing orthodoxy of their day. Of course, Jesus was a heretic, too. If we follow in his way, and insist on a healthy congruence between religion and spirituality, we should be prepared to be branded a heretic as well. Some of us have – or will be – shunned by our families. Some will be killed. This is just the way things are. As Jesus said in verse 105, "Whoever comes to know the father and the mother will be referred to as 'the son of a whore.'"

No one knows exactly what Jesus meant by "the father and the mother" in this verse. Gnostics no doubt connected "mother" with Sophia, while more orthodox Christians sometimes interpret her to be the Holy Spirit. For the purposes of this chapter, we might see the father as representing religious tradition and the mother as representing spirituality. Either of them is diminished if divorced, but together, such a marriage is sweet indeed. Yet a person who experiences a healthy balance between the two, who truly knows both father and mother will be called, "the son of a whore."

Again, Jesus is no doubt speaking from his own experience. Jewish tradition records that Jesus was born out of wedlock, the result of an illegitimate union between Mary, his mother, and Pandir, a Roman soldier (Talmud Shabbat 104b, Sanhedrin 67a). While this is possible (and perhaps the genesis of the virgin-birth stories), it is more likely that it is a rumor told by Jesus' detractors in order to discredit him. People fear anything they do not understand, and will seek to destroy what threatens them, just as they did Jesus. Jesus told a parable that illustrates this in graphic terms.

> "A just man had a vineyard, which he entrusted to some
> tenants that they might work in it, and yield for him its fruit.
> He sent his servant to collect grapes from the tenants of the
> vineyard. They grabbed his servant and beat him, and nearly
> killed him. The servant went and reported to his Lord. His
> Lord said, 'Perhaps they did not recognize him.' So he sent
> another servant. The tenants beat the other servant. Then
> the Lord sent his son, saying, 'Perhaps they will be ashamed
> before my son.' Because the tenants recognized the heir to
> the vineyard, they seized him and killed him. He who has
> ears should listen!" (65)

Note the resonance this story has with what we have been discussing. The just man is God, and the vineyard is Judaism. God entrusted the tradition to the Jewish people to yield fruit, or spirituality. But when prophets have been sent to gather up this fruit towards some purpose, they are savaged and beaten. So God sends one with whom God has a special relationship – presumably Jesus – whom they kill.

One cannot extend the metaphors in this story too far, though it is tempting to do so. In Thomas' gospel, Jesus is not depicted as the "Son of God" in the way that orthodox Christians understand that phrase, and one should not extrapolate such a meaning from the "just man's son" in the parable. If Jesus is God's child, Thomas implies, we are all God's children, with the same potential for divine communion Jesus himself enjoyed. There are no hierarchies in a universe that is One.

These distractions aside, however, the story is very clear: anyone claiming to have a message from God will be met with hostility from those who think they have it all figured out. This may be what prompted Jesus to say, in verse 66, "Show me the stone that the builders rejected; that is the cornerstone." It is tempting to meet the narrowmindedness of those who say, "Anyone with a new message must be wrong," with the equally shortsighted assertion, "Anyone with a new message must be right." Though Jesus does not go quite this far in verse 66, he does not stop very far shy of it. We do well to interpret this as another example of Jesus' hyperbolic statements – and he certainly does make his point.

Another example of his fondness for overstatement is found in verse 74, which provides a fit conclusion to our discussion of religion vs. spirituality. Though we do not know the context for this verse, we can imagine that Jesus has just witnessed a painful example of legalism triumphing over basic human compassion, such as when the Pharisees forbade the healing of a man on the Sabbath. Jesus must have rolled his eyes and prayed in exasperation, "Lord, there are many around the water fountain, but nothing in the well."

In our own day, as in his, many people come to religion in order to experience spirituality, true communion with the divine. We all gather around the well because we are all thirsty in our souls. That the well is dry is, once again, hyperbole – there is lots of water down there, we simply can't get at it. We are all waiting for someone with the authority to do so to lower a bucket. But as we shall see in the next chapter, no one can fetch that water for us.

Spiritual exercises

1. **Fire your God.** One of the greatest barriers to true spirituality is an image of God which is distorted or even harmful. Get our your crayons do a couple of drawings: first draw a picture of the God you were given as a child, then draw a picture of the kind of God you most want to be true. If you feel you have adequately captured these divergent deities,

do a ritual in which you, in effect, hand that old god "his" pink slip. In other words, *fire his ass.* You may want to express everything you want to say to this old god – and actually say it to the picture, including all the pain, anger, and resentment that has built up over the years. Then burn the picture and banish this god forever. Install the picture of the new God on an altar (if you do not have an altar set up somewhere in your home, this is a fine chance to erect one – place on it not just the picture, but objects or texts that call you to true communion).

2. **Take an inventory of practices, images, scriptures, music, etc.** Determine whether they help or hinder your goal of achieving a real and vibrant spirituality, or if they serve to keep you enslaved to unhelpful images and notions. Give each one a chance for "rehabilitation," asking, "What did this used to mean to me, when my religious understanding was such-and-such?" Then sit with it in meditation, asking the question, "What can this mean for me now, how can I understand it in a new way that will support me on my journey?" There are few objects or practices in almost any religion that cannot be remythologized, reimagined, and reinvigorated in positive and life-giving ways. Those that cannot be can be discarded, or set on a shelf until a new meaning is revealed to you. You may not have to wait very long!

The truth does not come from outside ourselves

I am ill and I long deeply for the health-giving draught
which Jesus Christ himself drank.
And he drank of it so deeply that he was on fire with love.
– Mechtild of Magdeburg (67)

Who can you trust? In a world filled with charlatans and hucksters, we ask this question of ourselves all the time. And nowhere does the fraud excel quite as much as in the realm of religion. Everywhere you turn you find someone else claiming to know the "truth," and many of them will even let you have it, for a price. Sometimes this price is monetary, sometimes it comes at the cost of one's unblinking loyalty or critical thinking. But there is always a price.

Just walking down the street today in Berkeley, I came across posters advertising three different gurus, each promising to grant enlightenment – for a workshop fee. The Roman Catholic church on the corner claims a monopoly on truth if you will promise your intellectual assent to every dogma proclaimed by the Vatican. And the Mormon church nearby also claims to be the one true church, but it will cost you 10% of your gross annual income to be a part of it. In addition to these, there are Zen roshis, Jewish rabbis, Course in Miracles study groups, and every manner of self-proclaimed prophet, each claiming to have "the truth."

Logically, of course, they cannot all be right, not in the way they claim. It is entirely possible that they each have a fragment of truth, that they are each, in their relative way, correct, and that they all point to a truth that transcends their individual traditions. But the more conservative practitioners of each tradition would reject this idea. Truth, for most religiously conservative traditions, is entirely proprietary.

We humans are hungry for truth. Life is difficult, dangerous, and uncertain, and we long for an ideological anchor which will afford us some stability. But it is very hard to know just whom we can trust. Who has true authority to speak to the Big Questions? Everyone who claims such authority gives different answers – can it be they are all charlatans? Or perhaps, are they simply self-deceived?

The Christian churches have certainly set Jesus up as the one with authority. In their teaching, Jesus divested himself of the power of godhood and took his place in the world to save it. He alone has the authority to answer the Big Questions. Even within the Gospel of Thomas we find people eager to place the mantle of authority upon Jesus. But, as we shall see, he always rebuffs their efforts.

In verse 91 his disciples said to him, "Tell us who you are, so that we may believe in you." Already, they were looking to invest authority in this man, to "believe in him," if he gave them the answers they wanted to hear. But Jesus recognized a trap when he saw it and rarely stepped into one. Instead, he answered them, "You read the face of the heavens and the earth, and yet you did not recognize the One who was in your presence; and you do not know how to read the present moment." The disciples were looking for an easy way – for someone to simply tell them the truth, but Jesus rejected this lazy man's path to enlightenment, telling them that everything they need to know (including the One that *is* the truth) has always been right in front of their noses, if only they had the eyes to see it, and were willing to do the work.

Again, in verse 52, the disciples try to tie Jesus to the authority of the Hebrew prophets, and said to him, "Twenty four prophets spoke in Israel, and they all spoke of you." But again, he rejected this kind of authority, and told them, "You have neglected the One who lives in your presence, and speak only of the dead." The prophets, like Jesus, only point to the truth, they are not themselves the truth. Jesus had only one small advantage over the prophets at this time – he was alive.

Some people apparently were even, at this early stage in Jesus' career, choosing to worship him. But he rebuked them as well, saying, "When you look upon the one who is not born of a woman, throw yourself on your face and worship him – for he is your Father" (15). Jesus, like everyone else, came forth mewling from the womb, and did not feel himself worthy of anyone's veneration.

Jesus is clear in these verses: he did not want anyone's faith, nor did he want anyone's worship. He was not asking anyone to believe in him, nor was he even asking anyone to believe a single thing he was saying – this is, in fact, just the opposite of what he wanted. Jesus was impatient with the attempts of nearly everyone around him to invest in him a status he did not claim for himself, and moreover, with people's desperate attempts to invest their faith in some external authority. What he wanted was something very different indeed. He wanted people to believe in *themselves*.

Embracing internal authority

In the early Baptist movement, only one doctrine held sway: that of "soul competency." This meant that no creed, no doctrine or dogma would be imposed on any believer, but instead that every person, every soul was competent to read the scriptures for him- or herself, and to come to his or her own conclusions about what was true. Early Baptists were held together not by common beliefs, but by a common freedom of belief and interpretation.

By the early 1960s when I was born, precious little was preached in Baptist churches about the doctrine of soul competency, and by the time I was a young man, the Southern Baptist churches had utterly rejected their heritage and imposed a dangerous and soul-killing fundamentalism. They had traded the freedom of the Gospel for the bondage of the Law, completely rejecting the admonitions of Paul to the contrary.

It was not until I had already left the Baptist church that I was even made aware of the doctrine of soul competency. But by then it did not matter – I had discerned within myself the same truth formerly enshrined by my Baptist forebears: all external forms of authority are but tyrannies dressed in religious garb, and none are to be trusted. In the end, I had to trust myself.

This is a very difficult thing to do, however. Most of us have been conditioned not to trust ourselves: we are told to trust our parents, and, when we are older, we transfer that paternal authority to the Catholic Fathers, or the rabbis, or some other religious authority. We are eager to trust anyone but ourselves. Yet this is exactly what the Jesus of Thomas is asking us to do.

When, in verse 13, Jesus asked his disciples to compare him with something, Thomas replied, "Master, my mouth is utterly incapable of saying what you are like." This is the right answer, but Jesus takes exception to how Thomas puts it, and he mildly rebuked him, saying, "I am not your master, because you have drunk and become intoxicated from the bubbling spring which I have measured out."

Jesus has become acquainted with Oneness, and has achieved unitive consciousness, and it is this consciousness that brings salvation and immortality. The Unity of all things is the truth, the "bubbling spring" that he has "measured out" in his teaching. Because Thomas has drunk of it – has received the teaching, internalized it, and has himself gained a glimpse of Oneness – he is not Jesus' inferior, but indeed, his peer. And this is Jesus' goal: not to gain followers or worshippers, but peers. Jesus "gets it," and he wants us to "get it" too; not so that we will venerate him, but so that we can enjoy life in the Kingdom even as he does.

He says this even more explicitly in verse 108: "Whoever drinks out of my mouth, he will become like me; I also will be as he is, and that which is hidden will be revealed to him." This is where the imagery of the "twin" comes into play. Thomas is Jesus' twin not simply because they were born at the same time of the same mother, but also because they share the same unitive consciousness. On the transpersonal plane, they are the same person, they are both the One, and thus they appear to us in phenomenal reality as twins.

But Thomas is not uniquely Jesus' twin – we are all called to become Jesus' twin, just like Thomas is. Of course, we cannot all be born of Mary, but we can all be "born again" into the same unitive consciousness Jesus knows and enjoys. In the scriptures of the early Jewish Christians we are told that those who accept Jesus' teachings do not worship Christ, but are themselves "Christs," giving light to the world.

In verse 24, it seems like the disciples are starting to "get it." They said to Jesus, "Show us to the place where you are, as it is necessary for us to seek it." Jesus answers them, "The one who has ears should listen! There is light existing in the inner person of light, which gives light to the whole world; anyone who does not become light is darkness." Note that Jesus is not saying that it is he who grants salvation in this verse, or that the light has some other external source. Instead he affirms that the light is in everyone, and that everyone has a choice as to whether they will own that light, to make it their own and bring it forth, to "become" that light. As Jesus said in verse 70, "When you bring forth that which is within you, that which you bring forth will save you. If you do not bring forth what is within you, that which you fail to bring forth will kill you." The light is in every one of us, but if we do not do the work to bring it forth, we are "darkness," and lost.

The truth, then, does not come from outside ourselves. The Buddha told his own disciples, "Do not be satisfied with hearsay or with tradition, or with legendary lore, or with what has come down in scriptures, or with conjecture or with logical inference, or with weighing evidence, or with liking for a view after pondering over it, or with someone else's ability, or with the thought 'The monk is our teacher.' When you know in yourselves: these things are wholesome, blameless, commended by the wise, and being adopted and put into effect they lead to welfare and happiness, then you should practice and abide in them" (Kalama Sutta).

Neither the Buddha nor the Jesus of Thomas wanted blind faith from their students. Both of them rejected the uncritical "authority" of the scriptures and the prophets and those who had set themselves up as "spiritual leaders," and pointed to the only true source of authority, the light within each and every person.

George Fox, the founder of the Quakers rediscovered this truth completely independent of both the Buddha and the Jesus of Thomas. Instead, he was – amazingly – able to glean from the doctored accounts in the Pauline gospels the essential truth of Jesus' original teaching. Quakers even today appeal to "the light within" as the final spiritual authority, and their services are not so much acts of worship as they are sessions for meditation, consciously bringing forth that which is within.

Anyone who succeeds in "bringing forth" his or her own light is, to Jesus' way of thinking, superior to those venerated by religious tradition. In verse 46, for instance, he said, "From Adam up to John the Baptist, there has been none among those begotten of women greater than John the Baptist, none who should not lower their eyes [in his presence]. But I say that whoever among you will become a little child, you will know the kingdom, and will be greater than John." As we have seen in previous chapters, "becoming a little child" is Jesus' way of describing the reclamation of unitive consciousness we all once enjoyed as infants. Thus, in the Kingdom, there are no hierarchies, no saints, no sinners, no prophets, no messiahs. Every being is filled with light, with truth, and either we choose to live into that truth or we don't. There are no judges, no juries, no condemnation, no blame – just fulfilled or unfulfilled potential. We either bring forth the light that is within us, or we do not.

Breaking free from the powers

All this is, of course, much easier said than done. It runs contrary to all our cultural and religious conditioning. Not only do we not trust ourselves, but we live in fear of those who would deign to wield spiritual power over us. But just as Eleanor Roosevelt said, "No one can make you feel inferior without your permission," just so, no one can wield authority over you without your leave.

In the Gnostic Christian system which flourished in the second and third centuries, the "authority" was the Hebrew God, Yaweh (whom they called by various names – we'll use "Samael," here). As the story goes, many ages ago, Sophia, God's Holy Wisdom, got curious, and wandered outside the "fullness" of God. Discovering she could not find her way back home, she tried to attain God by mimicking God. Since all God does is give birth, Sophia gave birth herself. But because she did not conceive with her consort, the Christ, the being she gave birth to was deformed.

This being, Samael, is therefore not the true God in the Gnostic system, but a lesser deity – the "blind god" – who nonetheless is the creator of this world. He set himself up as "God," and surrounded the earth with archons, evil angels whose job it is to refuse exit to the human souls seeking to escape this pain-filled world. He made Adam and Eve, and told them that he was the one and only deity, and that they must worship him alone.

But Sophia took pity on Adam and Eve, and placed within them a spark of true divinity – thus there was a part of them that was greater than their creator, and that longed to return to the fullness of the Divine. The true God also took pity on Adam and Eve and sent the Christ in the form of a serpent to open their eyes to their true situation, to reveal to them that Samael was only a pretender to the throne, and that their true home was not this world, but the world of light to which their souls long to escape. Once they were aware of their true plight, Samael's power over Adam and Eve was broken, and he could no longer hold them. Over time, the descendents of Adam and Eve forgot the liberating knowledge (gnosis) of their true plight. Thus, the Christ had to come again – this time in the form of Jesus of Nazareth – to repeat the message.

Many Gnostic groups existed as "secret circles" within orthodox Christian churches. When a member was deemed worthy to receive the "fullness" of the Gospel, he or she was told the truth: the god you have been worshipping is a fake, but there is another God who is good and true and who calls you to wholeness, to the place of light. The Gnostics devised various rituals or "sacraments" designed to break the power of Samael and his archons and liberate the soul.

We have already discussed one such ritual, the Bridal Chamber, in Chapter One. Another of these rituals was called, "Redemption," and it is indeed a great mystery. We do not know any details about this ritual, but we do know what it was supposed to do: break the power of the "Authorities," Samael and his evil angels, and to liberate one spiritually and psychologically from their tyranny. This ritual probably involved taking a symbol of this authority – perhaps a copy of the Ten Commandments – and ceremonially destroying it, thereby liberating a person from Samael's power.

Though there is no evidence that the Thomas school employed such a ritual, later Gnostics who valued the Gospel of Thomas certainly did, and it is indeed a powerful rebuke of tyrannical spiritual authority, and no doubt liberated those who performed it in a very real and profound way.

Even the myth itself is liberating, especially if we do not take it literally. It provided the roadmap for my own liberation once it occurred to me that Samael was the Southern Baptist god of my youth – not the true God, but a tyrannous pretender to the throne. I realized that fundamentalist religion was a form of spiritual bondage that sought to keep the souls and psyches of all humankind enslaved. But through the myth I also learned that there was another deity – the true God – that existed beyond the fundamentalist system, a good and worthy deity that called me to health and wholeness. It was to this true God that I owed my allegiance. This inspired me to reject the "official" sources of authority enshrined by the Baptist church and to develop my own internal spiritual compass. Indeed, I had to learn to trust my own inner light.

Resting in your own authority

It was probably these Gnostics who revered the Gospel of Thomas who are responsible for verse 50, where Jesus coaches his students on how to respond to those religious "authorities" who will undoubtedly challenge them. He told them, "If they say to you 'Where do you come from?' Say to them, 'We have come out of the light, the place where the light came of its own accord, and stood to his feet, and appeared to them in their own image.' If they say to you 'Is it you?' say, 'We are its children, and we are the chosen of the living father.' If they ask you, 'What is the sign of your father within you?' say to them, 'It is movement, and rest.'

This maps directly to the Gnostic myth just related above. The spark of true divinity Sophia placed within Adam and Eve is also in us, indeed, it is the birthright of all their descendents. There is, then, a part of us which has come out of the light, whose source is the fullness of the true divinity. And it is from this same fullness that the Christ came forth "of [his] own accord," who stood to his feet and appeared to us in our own image. We are not the light, but we are children of the light, and possessed of true relation to God.

Jesus posits another question, though: "What is the sign of your father within you?" The answer is curious: "Movement and rest." This harkens back to verse two, where Jesus said, "Let the one who seeks keep on seeking until he finds, and when he finds, he will be troubled, and if he is troubled, he will become surprised, and will become sovereign over all things." The Greek fragment discovered at Oxyrhyncus adds "...and then he will rest" to the end of this verse. All this seeking, finding, troubling, and reigning are all very "active," they are movements indeed. But all ends in rest. There is a lot of going forth, and much industry, but in the end the answer is found in sitting quietly by oneself. We may ask a lot of questions, we may go great distances in search of wisdom, we may exhaust ourselves with our internal wrestlings, but all is for naught if it does not lead us to the true authority, the "still small voice" (1 Kings 19:12) of the Spirit that whispers to all of us, the inner light glowing with hope in each and every breast. We all look for answers "out there," but if we are faithful, all our seeking will lead us back to ourselves, to the quiet and final authority in whom we find our only true rest.

Spiritual exercises

1. **Make a list of all the people or things you consider authoritative.** Just write them in random order, as they occur to you. (This should not be a short list.) Next, make another list, ordering the authorities found

in your first list according to their reliability – those at the top of the list should be those you regard as the most reliable of authorities, and those at the bottom as the least reliable. Note where your own conscience appears on this second list – if it appears at all! Finally, make a third list that represents your dream – what authority would you, in a perfect world, want to most honor? In what order do these authorities appear in your fantasy? Where does your conscience appear on this list?

2.   If you desire to be truly free from alleged spiritual authorities that have tyrannized you, or which prevent you from owning your own internal authority, you may wish to **perform the Gnostic sacrament of Redemption** for yourself. First, find a safe space in which to hold the ritual. It should be a private place where if feels okay to express any feelings that emerge. It is also good to have a witness to the event, someone with whom you feel safe, who is supportive of your spiritual process – perhaps a close friend, a therapist, or a spiritual director. For the ritual itself, find an object that represents the spiritual authority you want to be free of. If you are Catholic or Jewish or Wiccan, it may be a ceremonial goblet made of pottery, since each of these traditions utilize a goblet ritually. If you come from an Evangelical Christian background, you might want to use a Bible; if Mormon, a Book of Mormon or the Doctrine and Covenants. In any case, any object which represents the tyrannous spiritual authority will do. When you and your witness(es) are ready to begin, take a moment to become quiet and grounded. Then, address the spiritual authority directly, relating how you feel you have been hurt by his/her/their actions – you might find yourself speaking to a pastor or rabbi, or directly to the abusive deity. Once your feelings have been aired, rebuke the authority, revoking his/her/their hold on your life. Next, smash, burn, or rip apart the object that represents the authority. Feel free to let the pent-up rage out at this point, and really let the object have it. Once the rage has passed, light a candle to represent the light within you. Hold hands with your witness(es), and invoke those authorities you truly wish to honor, with the inner light having pride of place. Sit in silence until you have found a place of rest within yourself, then thank your witness(es) and close your circle.

We must be alone to be truly free

Listen to this divine call: You shall loose those
who are bound, you shall exhort the free, you
shall care for the broken, you shall enlighten and
teach, yet in all this you shall dwell alone.

— Mechtild of Magdeburg (125)

Marjorie sipped her tea and then stared into her cup for a long time. Finally she spoke again. "I know I should leave him – I *need* to leave him, but I just can't bring myself to do it. He's so abusive...."

I'd been concerned about her for a while, as she had seemed increasingly depressed, but this was the first I'd heard about abuse. I was instantly scared for her. "What do you mean? Has he hit you?"

"No, nothing like that." She pursed her lips and shifted in her seat. The other coffee shop patrons bustled about, and our table seemed the calm in the eye of a storm. "He's verbally abusive. I just don't know how much more I can take."

"I'm sorry," I said. "I didn't know it was so bad. I wish you'd called sooner." I said a silent prayer for her, and then asked, "What's keeping you from leaving him?"

She was silent for several minutes. I could see the wheels turning, and she made a couple of false starts. Finally, she said simply, "I can't bear the thought of being alone."

And there it was. The real reason, the true fear. Sure, there are some of us who are misanthropes, who prefer solitude to community, but most of us are social animals and crave the company of others, if only in measured doses. Marjorie is far from unique – for many people the fear of solitude is so great they will endure untold hardship to escape it. Yet the truth is, all community is ephemeral, and to some extent, illusory. The old saying, "We come into this world alone, and we leave the world alone," endures because it speaks a truth we all intrinsically know – and fear. Ultimately, it does not matter how many people we have gathered around us. The final walk will be made in our own company, alone.

Metaphysical solitude

We don't have to like it, we may be in denial about it, we might fight it – but we will still go out solo. Recall the Buddha's saying, "We suffer so long as we resist what is." If we are to avoid the extreme anxiety of such a prospect, we would do well to find a way to hold it that serves us, rather than living in thrall to an unnecessary and unrelievable fear.

The Jesus of Thomas gives us a way to do this. In verse 49, he tells us, "Blessed are those who are solitary and chosen, for you will find the Kingdom. For you come from it, and you will return to it again."

For those who live in the Kingdom – those who embrace unitive consciousness – solitariness is a given. If there is only One thing in the universe, then by necessity, that thing is alone, for there is no other. Once we have become that thing, and internalized our union with the all, we are utterly alone. Again, there is no other. Those who have discovered true solitude have found the Kingdom, they have become One.

This verse describes the primal myth found in almost every culture: from the One comes the many, and the many become One. According to Jesus, we all come from the Kingdom (Oneness) and we will return to it again. But we are blessed if we are conscious of this quest.

Embracing Oneness reveals to us the falsehood of "others," the illusion of all duality. Until we actually have an experience of such unity – and actually live in the Kingdom – such thoughts are no more than intellectual exercises. Previous chapters have addressed how to do this, but there are other aspects of solitude that bear consideration.

Internal solitude

The existential anxiety caused by the thought of our own impending death is often the catalyst that moves us to embrace spirituality. Alfred North Whitehead once wrote, "Religion is what the individual does with his own solitariness" (p. 16). The knowledge of our own going forth into Mystery unaided and alone is too terrible to bear. This fear of this solitude moves us to religion, but it is also the solitude we experience in the present, a foretaste of that great and eternal silence that creates the internal spaciousness in which true spirituality can take root and blossom.

Lao Tzu wrote, nearly three thousand years ago, "Thirty spokes join together at one hub, but it is the hole in the center that makes it operable. Clay is molded into a pot, but it is the emptiness inside that makes it useful. Doors and windows are cut to make a room, but it is the empty spaces that we use" (11). Without emptiness, silence, and solitude, there is no room for spirit, no experience of interiority. Whitehead explains further, "If you are never solitary, you are never religious. Collective enthusiasms, revivals, institutions, churches, rituals, bibles, codes of behavior, are the trappings of religion, its passing forms. They may be useful, or harmful; they may be authoritatively ordained, or merely temporary expedients. But the end of religion is beyond all this" (p. 17).

The end of religion is the soul alone with itself, and in contemplating this solitude we once again have a foretaste, a mytonomy, a symbol and foreshadowing of the solitude of the One, alone with itself forever. It is our own aloneness that creates the space to grow large inside, large enough to embrace and contain the All.

Wandering

For the early Thomas Christians, interior solitude was not sufficient to promote and achieve metaphysical solitude. They reinforced their process with social solitude, as well. While there is evidence of a Thomas community, there is also much material in its existing records that a goodly number of their members were peripatetic, itinerate preachers that roamed far and wide, carrying their unique gospel of enlightenment wherever they went. They considered such wandering to be an ideal which not everyone could embody, but was nonetheless held up as the best way of living out their faith. It is probably due to this ideal that the Thomas Gospel reached – and flourished – in Syria and faraway India.

In verse 86, Jesus speaks of his own itinerate life, when he said, "Foxes have their holes and birds have their nests, there. The son of man, however, does not have a place to lay his head and rest." Seeking to be like Jesus not only in his unitive consciousness, but also in his manner of life, the Thomas Christians followed his example. Nicholas of Cusa once wrote, "Eternal wisdom will not be obtained unless the possessor owns nothing" (37), and the Thomas Christians would most likely have agreed. They pointed to an imperative found in the Thomas gospel that is also the shortest verse in its pages: Jesus said, "Be passers-by" (42). That's the whole verse, yet pithy as it is, it speaks volumes about the kind of life the Thomas Christians revered. Accordingly, they did not stay long in one place, did not put down roots, did not get attached to the people or places they visited. It also implies an attitude toward earthly life itself: the believer is only passing through, and should not get too attached to anything in this world.

The Buddha, not surprisingly, espoused a similar ideal. He told his own disciples, "The person who wanders without a home in this world, leaving behind the desires of the world, and desires never return – I call this person a Holy Man" (Dhammapada 26:415).

The Thomas Christians did not just infer this mode of life from Jesus' teachings. He seems to have explicitly supported it himself. A verse in the Gospel of Thomas puts a surprising spin on a passage familiar from Luke's Gospel. According to Thomas' version, Jesus said, "The kingdom is like a shepherd who had a hundred sheep. The largest of these went astray. The shepherd left the other ninety-nine and looked for the one until he found it. He was very worried, and told the sheep, 'I love you more than the ninety-nine'" (107). In Luke's version, Jesus returns the lost sheep to the flock (15:4-7), but Thomas' sheep is not depicted as errant, but as uniquely deserving of favor, apparently *because* he has gone astray.

It seems that Jesus was supportive of the sheep that wandered, and was more pleased with wandering than with "following the herd" – further support for eschewing the kind of external authority we discussed in our last chapter. The sheep that the shepherd in this verse pursues is described as the "largest," but this could also be translated the "greatest." Jesus may have been saying that the best sheep is the one that goes his own way, heedless of the opinions and beliefs of the flock. It is that sheep that the shepherd (Jesus?) loves best and leaves the others behind to be with.

This parable has implications not only for supporting the itinerate life, but also for those who "wander" intellectually and spiritually. Jesus favors those who think for themselves, who do not simply mimic the beliefs handed to them by tradition, who do not "follow the flock" ideologically. This is yet another meaning of being "solitary," for instead of buying the party line, the favored sheep is the one with the courage to go his own way.

There are certainly advantages to the peripatetic life. A person who wanders is able to stay focused. Undistracted by employment, family, or societal responsibilities, she is able to single-mindedly keep her goal in mind. This is partly the justification used by the Roman Catholic Church for justifying clerical celibacy – without family, a priest is able to focus his full attention on his ministry.

Yet it would be wrong to overemphasize the ascetic nature of the Thomas Christians' practice. They did not sequester themselves in caves like the Desert Fathers and Mothers, or in cells as later monks and nuns were to do. Meister Eckhart wrote, "Asceticism is of no great importance" (58), and the Jesus of Thomas seems to have shared this opinion. When his disciples asked him about ascetic disciplines, he scorned them, saying, "If you fast, you will bring forth sin, and if you pray, others will condemn you, and if you give alms, you will create evil in your souls" (14). Instead, he proposed the itinerate ministry he so exemplified, saying, "And if you go into any land, and walk the territories, eat whatever people put in front of you. Heal the sick among them, for it is not what goes into your mouth that will defile you. Rather, it is what comes out of your mouth that will defile you." Mechtild of Magdeburg was just as vehement when she wrote, "Thus it is that those who would storm the heavenly heights by fierceness and ascetic practices deceive themselves badly. Such people carry grim hearts within themselves, they lack true humility which alone leads the soul to God" (76).

Jesus did not want his followers to withdraw into morbid seclusion or to waste their time with senseless mortifications. Instead he wanted them to cultivate an inner solitude, and, unencumbered, to take the good news of unitive consciousness wherever they went. He bid them not to eschew human contact, but to seek it out, to bring their message to as many as people as they could. He warned them not to get attached to the communities they visited, but to minister and heal those they found there, and then to move on. He probably would have agreed with Meister Eckhart's exhortation, "Spirituality is not to be learned by flight from the world, by running away from things, or by turning solitary and going apart from the world. Rather, we must learn an inner solitude wherever or with whomsoever we may be. We must learn to penetrate things and find God there" (90). The Thomas missionaries fled not from the world, but into it, eschewing not the world but senseless asceticism.

Modern wanderers

Wandering seems to be an ideal not only for the Thomas Christians, but unconsciously, perhaps by default, for us today as well. The Baby Boomers and Generation X are more peripatetic than any generations before them. We move more often, more easily, and further away than our grandparents would ever have dreamed. The days when people got a job out of college, and stayed there until retirement are long over – statistics indicate that most people now change jobs – and sometimes even careers – every five years or so. Nor are our home lives stable – over half of all marriages end in divorce, which no longer carries any discernible stigma except in the most fundamentalist of communities. We are not deeply connected to the land, to our work, or even, apparently, to each other, in sharp contrast to the way humankind has always lived. We do not set down roots, we *move*.

Because of this the itinerate ideal of the Thomas Gospel seems uniquely suited to postmodern life. In a world teeming with people, Jesus encourages us to cultivate inner solitude. In a culture where the only norm is constant change, Jesus does not shame our wandering, but favors it. In a world that encourages staggering diversity, Jesus invites us to dwell in the underlying unity that is hidden from us. But to do so, we will need to forsake the one thing our culture idolizes beyond all other gods: the ego.

Jesus said, "Whoever knows the All, but needs himself, needs everything" (67). Our attachment to the ego is the one thing that can undo us, no matter how much spiritual work we have done. This illusory self, the great tyrant, will stop at nothing to preserve its own sovereignty. Even if we have gained a glimpse of unitive consciousness, or in Jesus' words, even if we "know the All," so long as we cling to our ego, we are lost and undone by our need. We are not free.

And freedom – truly radical freedom – is the heart of Thomas' Gospel. Jesus seeks to set us free from illusion, from abusive and ineffectual religion, from the tyrannical ego, from everything that can bar us from enlightenment, from life in the Kingdom, from true intimacy with divinity. As Jesus said in verse 75, "There are many standing at the door, but the solitaries are the ones who will go in to the bridal chamber."

Just like my friend, Marjorie, we all hate to be alone. Yet in the Thomas Gospel Jesus reveals the profound and confounding truth that both isolation and community are illusions wrought by the phenomenal world. By embracing solitude, we paradoxically gain intimacy – and not the false intimacy of support groups, casual lovers, or fair weather friends, but the deep and abiding intimacy of Divinity above us, around us, and in us. For this is an intimacy that transcends both time and space, is both intrapersonal and transpersonal, is dependent upon no one, and yet is embracing of all.

If we find this intimacy, we find the Kingdom. If we flee this intimacy, it pursues us wherever we go. It is both evasive and inescapable. Call it the Kingdom or the bridal chamber, we can only go there alone – just like death. For it *is* a kind of death – the death of illusion, of duality, of ego. Mechtild of Magdeburg gives us provisions for our wandering when she says, "Love the nothing, flee the self. Stand alone. Seek help from no one. Let your being be quiet, be free from the bondage of all things. Free those who are bound, give exhortation to the free. Care for the sick but dwell alone. When you drink the waters of sorrow you shall kindle the fire of love with the match of perseverance. This is the way to dwell in the desert" (71).

Exercises

1. **Do some writing** to get in touch with your fear of being alone. Look back on the choices you have made to both be alone and to avoid being alone, and evaluate the wisdom of those choices, taking full advantage of the luxury of hindsight. Note how you have sabotaged potentially fruitful opportunities for solitude, and discover the fears and assumptions that drove you. Write another paragraph about your fears in the present: how do you avoid solitude, and why?

2. **Schedule opportunities for fruitful solitude.** Interior spaciousness does not just appear some morning with your cereal and newspaper. It must be cultivated with care and attention. Instead of putting on music or the TV automatically, let the silence simply **be**. Instead of finding something to do, do nothing. Instead of rifling through your address book for a friend to do things with, do them by yourself. Pay

attention to how anxious this makes you, what fears or psychological pain results, and write a few paragraphs about it.

3. As we wander enough in our culture, we can do further wandering in our minds. **In your imagination, sever yourself** from the people, places, and things you love. Ask yourself, "Who am I without them?" and write down what comes to you.

4. **Take a vacation by yourself** – the longer the better – and set off with no destination in mind. See where your wandering leads you. Resist the urge to "do" things when you stop. Eschew the marketplace and village for the trees and the quiet. Look for signs and portents wherever you go – for if you look for them, they will appear. Keep a log of these "messages" and ponder their possible meanings.

Screw the system, but love your body

From craving arises sorrow and from craving arises fear.
If a man is free from craving, he is free from fear and sorrow.

– The Buddha, *Dhammapada*, 16:216

I belong to a very unusual church that, while being theologically liberal, uses, of all things, the *1662 Book of Common Prayer* liturgy. I admit to loving the Jacobean language; it creates a feeling of sacred space, and serves to usher one into the Mystery. Unfortunately, those early Anglican liturgists responsible for the Prayer Book were possessed of some rather destructive theologies, which most of us are aware of from our own experience in the church, whatever denomination we might have experience with. There are several lines that, as a layperson, I would be glad to just skip, but as clergy I must, as it were, bite the bullet and spit them out.

One of the lines that really sticks in my craw comes at the point in the service when we ask those who have birthdays or anniversaries to come forward for a blessing. As part of this "blessing" we ask God to keep them "unspotted from the world."

At first this really got my dander up. It reminded me of the traditional Western way of viewing nature as something malevolent, something that must be beaten back and subdued; of centuries of cowering humans living in fear of the big bad "world" that might at any time devour them. We have seen the disparaging results of such a way of viewing the world – in environmental destruction, and an aggressive industrialism – and saying such a line leaves a bitter taste in my mouth.

This way of thinking about nature goes back to the Christian Gnostics of the second century, who viewed the world as a corrupt and evil place. They thought that humans have within them the spark of true divinity from the alien God far away in the Pleroma. This world is a prison planet, and not our true home at all.

Since our only complete copy of the Gospel of Thomas comes to us after centuries of use in Gnostic Christian communities it is hard to tell whether some of its verses – especially those that seem to disparage the world – are original to Jesus or are later Gnostic interpolations into the text. How are we to understand such troublesome verses as 56: "Whoever has come to know the world has discovered a corpse, and whoever has found a corpse, the world is not worthy of him" without resorting to a Gnostic dualism that demonizes the created order and is at odds with the unitive teachings of Jesus in Thomas' Gospel?

In wrestling with how to deal with this seemingly dualistic prayer in our liturgy, I finally pulled out my Greek New Testament and lexicons in an effort to "re-mythologize" the line for myself, to gain a greater understanding of what Jesus might have meant when he spoke of overcoming "the world. "

What I found was most enlightening, indeed. The Greek word usually translated "world" is *kosmos,* and refers not to the natural world, the Earth, but to the political world, the hierarchy, the "order," or in its most appropriately pejorative English equivalent, the "system."

Eschewing the "system"

It was not the "natural order" with which Jesus had his beef, but with the religio-political order, the pecking order, the tyranny and ruthlessness of those who wield power. Thus, when Jesus says,

"What does a person gain by winning the whole world at the cost of one's soul?" (Mark 8:36) we are able to understand. It is not the Earth that is in opposition with our true nature, that which is good, humble, and innocent; but rather the "system," which is set up as a power over others in the hands of a few.

This revelation of the true meaning of the "world" is invaluable when seeking to understand the Thomas Gospel. There are many verses that appear, at first glance, to disparage – even demonize – the created order. Yet this interpretation contradicts the theology of Thomas. A true theology of unity does not split parts off and demonize them. There can be no false distinctions between "holy" and "corrupt," "sacred" and "profane." The spirit cannot be "good" and the flesh "evil," or unity has no meaning and has degenerated into meaningless dualism.

But if we understand "the world" to refer not to the created order but to the "system," these enigmatic verses in Thomas suddenly come to life. In verse 27, Jesus said, "If you do not fast from the world, you will not find the kingdom. If you do not make the sabbath a sabbath, you will not look upon the Father." In this verse, Jesus is not asking us to pursue an ascetic life secluded from society; he is instead insisting that those who follow in his way eschew the power games and manipulation of people so common among those in power, both secular and religious. He insists instead that we fast from "the system," that we extricate ourselves from the Machiavellian machinations that drive so much of society, stand apart from those who abuse others in order to get their own way. For if we cannot stop seeing other people as objects, as pawns whose sole purpose for being is to further our own selfish ends, we cannot be enlightened, we cannot enter the Kingdom.

In other words, this verse is not about fasting from food, but about fasting from power. The exercise of power, no matter how well intentioned, leads inevitably to its abuse. In my experience, this is a universal law, and from it no one is exempt. The greatest tragedy is that the "system" is not limited to secular politics, but, as many of us who have worked for years in spiritual communities know so well, the "system" is also alive and active in our spiritual arenas.

Many of us have broken away from churches or organizations that have abused us in the past, and have embraced new churches or organizations which we hoped would bring us nurturing and acceptance, only to feel betrayed when the same politicking and power-dealing rears its head again. As Sam Keen writes, "the spiritual revolution has a problem of new tyrannies. Haven't we seen enough corpses and failed gurus around in the last twenty years to remind us to be careful? Don't we have reincarnated Buddhist holy men knowingly passing AIDS to people they sleep with? Don't we have the worst kind of tyranny in almost every organization that becomes more and more 'spiritual?' There is a principle at work here: The more we want to rise into the light, the more the shadow, the more the evil comes and gets us from behind."

Yet the grasping after power is a form of desire, and as the Buddha has so eloquently taught us, it is desire which causes suffering. Desire can be conquered, power can be eschewed, and suffering can cease. As the Buddha wrote, "Whoever in this world overcomes his selfish cravings, his sorrow falls away from him, like drops of water from a lotus flower" (Dhammapada 24:336).

Of all the selfish cravings we human beings experience, none is more dangerous than that for power. There is no intoxicant known to humankind more addictive or corrupting than the wielding of power over another. In verse 28 Jesus said, "I stood to my feet in the midst of the world, and outwardly I appeared to them in the flesh. When I came upon them, they were all drunk, and I did not find any of them thirsty. And my soul grieved for the children of humanity, for their minds are blind, and they do not see. For they have come into the world empty, and they seek to leave it empty. But now they are drunk; when they sober up, they will have a change of heart."

Jesus appears a little too optimistic in this verse, in my opinion. It takes a great jolt to disabuse an addict of his or her substance of choice, and power is among the worst. His description of their intoxication and careless disregard for truth seems right on target, but what could possibly move them to "sober up" and have a "change of heart"? Such sobriety is obviously not going to happen on a grand scale. As Jesus said in verse 23, "I will choose you, one out of a thousand and two out of ten thousand, and they will stand to their feet as one." Jesus is not trying to convert the masses, but to find those few select souls who have themselves been wounded by the abuse of power – both political and spiritual – and are therefore ready to relinquish its corrosive influence.

In verse 56, Jesus tells us in no uncertain terms the "value" of the "system": "Whoever has come to know the world has discovered a corpse, and whoever has found a corpse, the world is not worthy of him." Reading "the system" for "the world," this verse is a powerful warning. Whoever has become acquainted with the system has become involved in a corrupt and evil organism, a thing devoid of any real life, a dead thing. But the good news is that those few people who can recognize that the system is corrupt are superior to it, and not necessarily bound to it or controlled by it.

To paraphrase the Buddha, "When a man considers this 'system' as a bubble of froth, and as the illusion of an appearance, then the king of death has no power over him. Come and look at this 'system.' It is like a royal painted chariot wherein fools sink. The wise are not imprisoned in the chariot" (Dhammapada 13:170-171). The system is not eternal, it is a bubble of froth that is here today and gone tomorrow. Every system of oppression will fall, and one tyrant will give way to another as those who live by the sword die by the same.

Jesus' answer to this rat race is to simply opt out, to refuse to play such games. In verse 110 he tells us, "Whoever has found the 'system' and become rich, let him renounce the 'system'." Such riches come at too high a cost: the dehumanization of those "pawns" who do our bidding, the objectification of others, the addictive intoxication of power, and the dualistic illusion of "us" (or more accurately, "me") vs. "them" that renders unitive consciousness – and thus any real freedom – impossible. A high price, indeed.

In Luke's Gospel we read the story of the rich young ruler, who approaches Jesus and asks what he must do to gain eternal life (18:18). To his extreme horror Jesus tells him the one thing he does not want to hear: "Go, sell all you have and give the money to the poor, and come follow me."

What Jesus is really asking for is a radical trust in the universe – a faith that God will take care of us even if we relinquish the power and security we have. He asks us to forsake "the system," and trust that we will be provided for anyway.

He asks a lot, and of all the exercises and shifts in consciousness required by the Way of Thomas, this is the hardest. This is the true test that separates the sheep from the goats. Who among us is willing to part with our privilege? Who can bear to part with what meager amount of power or wealth or influence he or she has gained, whether it is little or great? And yet we must, if we are to awaken to our deepest and most authentic selves.

The body

If who we truly are is the universe itself, then what are we to make of our bodies? The Gnostic prejudice against the world was applied with equal vehemence against the body as well. As products of this world, the body is married to it, a part of it, and as such, utterly irrideemable. Thus the Gnostics taught that Jesus was not a human being at all but an emissary from the alien world of the true God. He did not have a body at all, since the true God can have nothing to do with corrupt matter. Instead, he merely seemed to have a body, but it was really an illusion. (Jesus' statement in verse 28, quoted in our previous section, seems to suggest a Gnostic interpolation to this effect: "I stood to my feet in the midst of the world, and outwardly I appeared to them in the flesh....")

Gnostics generally took one of two approaches to the body. Since it was corrupt and of little importance anyway, many felt it did not matter what they did with it, and might as well use it as a ritual vehicle to aid them in escaping the world. These became the libertine Gnostics, whose orgiastic rites were both scandalous and legendary. We have already mentioned the Gnostic Bridal Chamber ritual (see Chapter One), a fairly benign libertine ritual. More titillating are the reports found in the writings of the heresiologists of the early church, one of which recounts the tale of a bishop who, while traveling, was pleased to find hospitality amongst a group of Christians in a strange city. But this pleasure quickly turned to disgust as the bishop witnessed precisely what sort of "love feast" was being celebrated. As Epiphanius, writing about 375, reports,

> The wretches have intercourse with one another...in the passion of illicit sexual activity, then they lift up their blasphemy to heaven. The woman and the man take the male emission in their own hands and stand gazing toward heaven with the impurity in their hands; and of course they pray...offering what is in their hands aptly to the parent of the entirety. And they say, "We offer unto you this gift, the body of Christ," and then they eat it, partaking of their own filthiness. And they say, "This is the body of Christ, and this is the Passover because of which our bodies feel passion and are constrained to confess the passion of Christ." And likewise with the woman's emission: when it happens that she has her period, her menstrual blood is gathered and they mutually take it in their hands and eat it. And they say, "This is the blood of Christ" (26.4.4-8; Bentley Layton, *The Gnostic Scriptures*, 206-7).

Not all Gnostics were so lascivious in their approach to the body. The other approach was that of the ascetics, who, viewing the body as a vile thing to be escaped as soon as possible, gave its corrupt desires no quarter. They mortified their flesh, eschewed all sexual contact and every pleasure in hopes of decreasing the hold of the flesh over them.

It is this ascetic approach to the body that was to be most influential on the Christian religion. St Augustine spent eleven years as an ascetic Manichean Gnostic, and when he converted to orthodox Christianity (and subsequently became the foremost theologian in the church's history) he unfortunately brought the Gnostic bias against the flesh and the world into the church, even while professing to argue against such "errors."

Just as an alcoholic colors all the world with his or her own addiction, and refuses to believe that anyone can drink responsibly (because he or she cannot), just so Augustine, a sex addict, colored all the world with his own addiction, and bequeathed to the future of the Christian church a world-denying, flesh-mortifying doctrine that has been disasterous for an uncountable multitude of people. Because Augustine could not deal appropriately with his own sexual neuroses the Gnostic hatred of the world and the flesh was allowed to infect the teaching of the Christian church, and it continues to color our experience even today.

The Gospel of Thomas betrays a similar disdain for the body, and once again we cannot be sure if these verses are original to Jesus or are later Gnostic interpolations. Verse 29 seems to support the Gnostic myth that portrays Sophia as placing within Adam and Eve the spark of true divinity (recounted in Chapter Six): Jesus said, "If the flesh came into being because of the spirit, it is a wonder. If spirit came into being because of the body, however, it is a wonder of wonders. Instead, I am amazed at this: how such great richness has come to dwell in such poverty."

In this verse Jesus marvels that the spark of true divinity, the spirit, has come to dwell in the poverty of the body. This is surely an example of Gnostic dualism that honors the spirit at the expense of the body. Yet Jesus does not rule out the possibility that the spirit derives from the body and not the other way around. It may be that he is not demonizing the body, just expressing wonder that such a marvelous creature as the spirit could derive and find a home in a vehicle that is so very limited, and must eventually succumb to death and decay.

Buddhism seems to be able to hold this tension between body and spirit with more equanimity. Hsuen-sueh wrote, "The body is the tree of enlightenment, the mind is like a bright mirror. Constantly take care to wipe it clean: don't let it be defiled with dirt and dust" (Blue Cliff Record, 185). This Zen teacher seems to suggest that the body is not the source of the dirt and dust, but instead honors the body as "the tree of enlightenment," the only vehicle and foundation for enlightenment that we have. We should seek to keep the mind (or the spirit) clean of illusions, but such diligence does not come at the expense of the body – it is the body that makes possible the liberation of the mind. Both body and mind are valuable, both are needed to achieve enlightenment.

Yet this seems to be contradicted by the Jesus of Thomas. In verse 112 he says, "Woe to the flesh that depends on the soul, and woe to the soul that depends on the flesh" and again, in verse 87, "Wretched is the body that depends on a body, and wretched is the soul that depends on these two."

On the one hand these verses seem to support the ideal of self-sufficiency discussed in our previous chapter. A healthy body ought not need rely on the doggedness of spiritual will to endure, nor the spirit depend upon something as ephemeral as the body. But perhaps that is Jesus' point – if indeed these verses are original to Jesus – being human is often a dangerous affair, for whom woe is never far away. Perhaps wretchedness is simply the human condition, and Jesus, with typical candor, was simply pointing this out. Such wretchedness is not the same as Calvin's "depravity," for it does not point to a sickness borne of sin but simply the precarious vulnerability of embodied life. Jesus may not be saying that it should be otherwise, only that sorrow is the unavoidable lot of the living. To say, "life is hard" is not to cast derision on life, but only to honestly face it. Just so, the dance of body and spirit is often a woeful choreography in which we are nonetheless privileged to participate.

On the other hand, this verse may simply be another dismissal of duality. Any body that needs a spirit (as if they were two things) is a sad thing, for it is trapped in illusion. Likewise, any spirit that requires a body – and cannot see through the illusion of duality – is equally wretched. Body and spirit are not two things, but only perceived aspects of the One.

Both readings may be useful for us, since though unitive consciousness is the goal towards which we strive, most of us also have to fight traffic, fix dinner, floss our teeth, and otherwise navigate the phenomenal universe which is, to all appearances, very dualistic indeed. Until we gain an experience of unity, such talk is entirely academic, which is why practice is so terribly vital.

The most disparaging and, frankly, distressingly dualistic verse is the last one in the entire collection, number 114. This is the verse that most angers women, in particular, and is troublesome to most everyone. In it, Simon Peter is reported to have said, "Let Mary depart from us, for women are not worthy of Life."

But Jesus answered him, "Behold, I will lead her, and I will make her male so that she might also be a living spirit like you males. For any woman who makes herself male, she will enter the Kingdom of heaven."

As it stands, this verse comes across as horribly misogynistic. The Gnostic dualism that we have seen honoring Heaven over the earth, and the spirit over the body here honors men over women. While this is fine Gnosticism, it is very poor Thomas theology. A good argument could be made for this being simply a Gnostic interpolation, and it is tempting to dismiss it as such and simply move on. But I believe this verse to be original to Jesus and part of the early redaction of the Thomas Gospel – it is simply incomplete.

I believe that this verse originally recorded Jesus as saying, "Behold, I will lead [Mary], and I will make her male so that she might also be a living spirit like you males. For any woman who makes herself male, she will enter the Kingdom of heaven. *And any man who makes himself female will likewise enter the Kingdom.*"

I realize it is bold to suggest the addition of a text that survives in no version of the Gospel, nor even in any secondary sources, yet such a reading is entirely congruent with the theology of Thomas as described in verse 22: "When you make the two into one...and when you make the male and the female into a single one, so that the male is not male and the female is not female...then you will enter the Kingdom." Such an explanation makes instant sense of the verse, consistent with the Gospel's internal logic, and at the same time refutes the Gnostic dualism suggested by the verse as it appears.

Jesus' remark, "I will make her male so that she might also be a living spirit like you males," makes more sense when delivered with a wink, a sarcastic nod to the male disciples' own misguided sense of superiority which Jesus does not for a moment accept, yet which he knows his followers possess. He can only shatter one illusion at a time, after all, and that only if he is lucky.

Assuming my reading is correct, the second half of this verse seems to have been omitted by an early scribe, probably because of his own misogyny (or, more likely, the misogyny of the culture of which he was a part). The second half of the verse may have simply been too threatening, and out of some misguided attempt to correct what Jesus *must* have meant, or to defend his own embattled feelings of machismo it was easier to simply omit the text than it was to deal with it. This early scribe's attempt to avoid the hard saying of Jesus thus created an even harder saying for those of us who have come after, who do not share the misogynistic proclivities of the scribe.

Yet the restored verse is a wonder. No woman can be whole, can enjoy true unity until she has fully embraced her own masculinity, thus eradicating her own internal dualism. And likewise, no man can be whole without embracing his femininity. This insight has deep resonance with later Jewish mysticism. In the *Zohar*, Rabbi Shim'on is reported to have said, "Supernal mysteries are revealed in these two verses: 'Male and female He created them,' making known the Glory on high, mystery of faith. Out of this mystery, Adam was created. 'Male and female He created them.' From here we learn: Any image not embracing male and female is not a supernal, true image. Come and see: the blessed Holy One does not place His abode anywhere male and female are not found together" (21).

Ever since the 1960s counter-culture, Western society has been moving toward an androgynous ideal. The hippie movement legitimated trousers for women and long hair for men. The gender-bending of pop idols in the 1970s, along with the increasing visibility and acceptance of gay and lesbian people in the 1980s further raised public consciousness. Today few men strive to be insensitive, and even fewer women are eager to be disempowered. We have, as a culture, begun to shed centuries of Gnostic dualism, entrenched machismo, and gender prejudice.

The Jesus of Thomas does not disdain the world or the body, but he does rail against the "system," which seeks to keep us enslaved to dualistic perception. Any "system" which honors the sky over the earth, the spirit over the body, the rich over the poor, men over women, or any other dualistic distinction is counter-productive to the goal of enlightenment. The world is a fine stage on which to act out our drama of reconciliation, yet we must be mindful that it is ephemeral and not get too attached to it. Likewise, as the Buddha so wisely bore witness, the body is the only vehicle for enlightenment that we have and we do well to cherish it and care for it with the same zeal that we often reserve for the health of the spirit. For the body and the spirit are not two things, but one. Likewise heaven and earth, and male and female are not distinct in fact, but only in appearance.

The Way of Thomas disparages none at the expense of any other. It eschews the system – and the lies of duality upon which it rests, but embraces the world, body and spirit. If we are to discover oneness, we must do the same.

Exercises

1. The distinction between "the world" and "the system" is crucial. As an exercise in irony, pursue oneness by making distinctions: **create two lists,** one of which lists those aspects of the world that are part of the created order, even if they are not necessarily things you like (for instance, everyone likes sunsets, but only a few of us like spiders or snakes, yet each are part of creation). Then make another list of those things that are part of the "system," even those things which you do like (everyone hates systematized oppression, for instance, but some of us quite like TV commercials when they are funny or poignant). These lists can become unwieldy rather quickly, so it is not as important to be comprehensive as it is to be representative. Once the lists are complete (or you are satisfied that you have a good representation and enough to work with), cross off those items which you feel you can truly embrace, or that you would like to truly embrace. Look at what is left over on both lists. What items on the list of the "world" do you need to do work on in order to truly internalize them? What items on the list of the "system" are aspects of human nature that you simply don't like yet need to embrace anyway? (For instance,

the ancient scribe who was scared of his own femininity would have done well to do some work in this area.) What items are truly obstacles to oneness? Which are merely uncomfortable or hard, and which items are truly harmful and dualistic?

2. The Hindu tradition has developed many powerful tools to help people see through the illusion of duality. One of them is the ancient admonition, "Tat tvam asi," which means, "you are that." The Hindu knows that whatever he or she beholds is in reality him- or herself, and repeating "Tat tvam asi" is an effective discipline to help one internalize this truth. **Practice** going about your day, **saying to yourself, "I am that,"** in reference to everything you encounter. This is a difficult practice to maintain, but can be very effective when practiced with careful intention even for brief periods. Try it on your commute to work, or while out shopping. For every person you encounter, every grisly accident scene, every pile of dog feces, every rusted fender, every homeless person, every Machiavellian power luncher the mantra is the same: "You are that." Because you *are*.

3. Meditate upon the ways in which you are defined by gender roles. If you are a woman, ask yourself what personality traits society generally regards as masculine, and how you appropriate or eschew such behaviors. Likewise, if you are a man, what personality traits generally thought of as feminine do you embrace or reject? Write down those traits you typically avoid, and meditate on – or pray about – these items. How would embracing these behaviors help you to be a more whole person? What discomfort arises in you around some of the items, and why? If you are heterosexual, engage in some active imagination, and fantasize about making love to someone of your own gender. If you are homosexual, do the same regarding someone of the opposite gender. If this is uncomfortable, stick with it until you feel yourself desensitized. The object here is not to change anyone's sexual orientation, but instead to help dissolve the illusory distinctions between male and female, masculine and feminine, homosexual and heterosexual. In truth, gender is only about reproductive equipment, sexual roles, however, are a product of society, the "system," and as such are illusions – the power of which must be broken if we are to be free.

Jesus is a mystery,
(and so is everyone else)

"Who do you say that I am?"

So, who was Jesus? What was Jesus' own opinion of himself and his mission? Was he God, a man, or something in between? Jesus himself asks this question of the disciples in the Gospel of Matthew, "Who do you say that I am?" (16:15). This is a hard question to answer because every report we have – the many gospels and letters from antiquity – are written by someone with a theological agenda. Jesus is always seen through the ideological lens of the scribe reporting events, so that it is often difficult to separate the wheat from the chaff – the propaganda from the event. It is tempting to think that if we could just go back to the first century, closer to the source, we might find an answer.

Yet even in the first century, followers of Jesus could not agree on these questions. As we discussed in the introduction, debate raged amongst the many early Christian communities about just who Jesus was and why he came. Through the centuries councils have made decrees, opinions have been coerced by the sword, and confessions have been issued by various communities claiming to know the "true" character and mission of Jesus. Even the four gospels contained in the Christian Bible do not agree – each of them portray Jesus from a different perspective, and cast him in a different light. In Matthew, he is a prophet sent to Israel, in Mark he is a rebel, in Luke he is the ideal man, and in John, he is God, plain and simple.

The Gospel of Thomas is helpful in this search because it provides another early witness to the Jesus event. It still is written from a particular theological perspective, but it also seems to contain earlier and more reliable reports than even the canonical gospels. This does not mean that Thomas should be read uncritically – indeed, a critical reading is the only sane way to approach any text, even (and perhaps especially) scriptures. What does the Gospel of Thomas say about Jesus and his mission?

Jesus' ministry

Jesus certainly believed that in his teaching, he was bringing a message of great importance. He told his disciples, "I will give to you what eyes have never seen, what no ear has heard, what hands have not touched, and what has never arisen in the human heart" (17). This is hyperbole, of course, but, as we have seen, Jesus is fond of overstatement (such as when he tells us we must hate our parents in verses 55 and 101), so this should not concern us too much. He employed this technique frequently in his teaching – but, unfortunately, his is a teaching that rubs almost everyone the wrong way.

Unlike many contemporary liberal Christians, who would have Jesus be a non-violent peace activist in the mold of Gandhi, Jesus is quite clear that his teaching will cause nothing but trouble. In verse 16 he tells us, "Perhaps people are thinking that I have come to cast peace upon the world. What they do not know is that I have come to cast division upon the earth – fire, sword, war. For there will be five people in a house, and three of them will be against the other two, and two against the three; the father will be against the son, and the son against the father; and they will stand to their feet, alone."

Jesus knows that his message is a radical one. As we have seen in previous chapters, his perspective is very much at odds with the religious establishment of his day, and very threatening indeed to those invested in that tradition. The irony is that his vision is a mystical one of cosmic unity, and yet in the field of human relations it will cause nothing but division and strife.

That Jesus is conscious of this irony is evident in verse 72. "A man said to Jesus, 'Speak to my brothers so that they may divide my father's belongings with me.' He answered him, 'Mister, who made me a divider?' He turned to his disciples, and said, 'Honestly, am I a divider?'" One can imagine that Jesus is saying this with a wry grin and a wink – it is, in fact, the funniest verse in Thomas, and he is using this opportunity for a little in-joke with his disciples. His message is one of unity – or more precisely, of unitive vision – and yet everywhere he goes it sows division.

This is evidence that Jesus was keenly aware of the subtleties of his message, and its consequences. He knows he is outside of the mainstream of Jewish teaching, and he fearlessly faces this.

"I have cast fire upon the world," he tells us in verse ten, "and see, I am tending it until it burns." Jesus is also aware of the power of a single idea to change the world. Today cognitive scientists speak of "memes," ideas that have a life of their own, and like a virus, "infect" populations as the idea moves through one society after another. Jesus seems to understand that he has released a meme upon the world – he has, to borrow the imagery of another culture's mythology, opened Pandora's box.

Notice he speaks in the past tense. The cat is already out of the bag. The deed is done. The teaching is out there. He is simply tending the blaze until it envelopes the world. It doesn't matter if he lives or dies, if he is murdered or lives a long life. It is not Jesus that is important, but the teaching. And the teaching is *out there*.

Jesus understands that he is not only putting himself in harm's way by bucking the system to such a degree. He also knows, as we have just seen, that this teaching is going to cause problems for his students, too. But he is concerned to encourage them in spite of this. "Whoever is near me is near the fire," he tells them in verse 82, "and whoever is far from me is far from the kingdom." The fire he speaks of here might be one of comfort. Itinerate preachers walking from town to town know well the warmth and comfort a fire provides, and this saying no doubt elicited warm and fuzzy feelings in Jesus' inner circle. They have known many a night gathered around a blazing fire with their teacher.

This understanding might also apply not to Jesus himself, but to his teachings. This interpretation is supported by a very similar passage that would later appear in the Talmud:

> "From His right hand went forth a fiery law for them" [Duet 33:2]. The words of Torah are compared to fire, for both were given from heaven, and both are eternal. If a man draws near the fire, he derives benefit; if he keeps afar, he is frozen, so with the words of the Torah: if a man toils in them, they are life to him; if he separates from him, they kill him.
>
> (Sifre Deuteronomy 143a)

Just so, those who engage with Jesus' teaching find life, warmth, and comfort, and those who distance themselves from it or reject it reject the Kingdom of which he is herald.

Yet this verse may be read with a negative aspect as well. It may mean that whoever is near Jesus – whoever follows the path of Jesus, the path of mystical insight – is asking for nothing but trouble, and will hence be "near the fire."

But he also tells them, in a neat parallelism, that the alternative is no alternative, for if you are far from Jesus – if you do not try to grasp his teaching – you are, again, far from the Kingdom, from enlightenment and salvation. Jesus assures the disciples that his way is not an easy one. To internalize his teaching will cause one great strife, but he also promises that it comes with great rewards.

The consequences of following this teaching are painful not only for his disciples, but it appears to have been quite painful for Jesus himself, as well. In the biblical gospels it is very clear that Jesus' teaching is not accepted by the majority of people he meets. This is especially true of those who knew him as a child. Though the

Gospel of Thomas contains no extended narratives that give us a sense of his reception, hints of it are still visible. In verse 31 he says, "No prophet is accepted in his own village; no physician heals those who know him." This is probably a very reliable tradition as we find it both in Thomas and in the biblical witness.

Anyone who has "made good" and tried to go home again understands the unique pain alluded to here. People who have seen you scuff your knees and caught you with your hand in the cookie jar are loathe to erect much of a pedestal for you. Even though Jesus is not looking to be exalted in any way, it has still got to hurt that the people he knows and loves the most cannot truly hear him. He would always be "Joseph's son" (John 6:42), never "rabbi" to people in his own village.

I am sure that none of this came as much of a surprise to him, but Jesus was probably not prepared for the level of vitriol aimed at him. In verse 105, he says, "Whoever comes to know the father and the mother will be referred to as 'the son of a whore.'" This verse bears much unpacking. It is likely that Jesus is speaking of himself, here. While it was not unusual to refer to God as masculine, "the father," to speak of divinity as feminine, "the mother" would smack of paganism and would have been considered heresy.

But later Gnostic Christians would also speak of a divine feminine, Sophia, who is sometimes referred to as "the mother." Though this verse may be a later Gnostic interpolation, it is congruent with the teaching of Thomas' Jesus. Anyone who knows the balance, the yin and yang, the father *and* the mother and the larger unity in which they coinhere will – if they are mad enough to speak of it – open themselves up for derision.

Jesus was probably also quite used to being considered a bastard. If there is any truth in the infancy narratives of the biblical gospels, Mary his mother got pregnant before she was married. As we saw in Chapter Five, the Talmud records the memory of the mainstream Jewish opinion of him – that he was an illegitimate child of an adulterous affair between Mary and a Roman soldier, named "Pandira." The name of the soldier reported to be Jesus' father in this passage is a joke, kind of like "Naughtius Maximus" in Monty

Python's *Life of Brian*, as "Pandira" means "Panther" and is probably a reference to his sexual prowess.

The implication of this verse, however, is that such stories did not start to circulate until after Jesus began teaching his "heretical" message. It is easy to see how people who were threatened by his ideas would turn to slander to discredit him in the eyes of the masses. It may be that the tradition of his illegitimacy actually starts here, and has no foundation in history. If this is the case, it was a widespread rumor, as it would be incorporated and explained by the biblical gospel writers.

This teaching was challenging then not only for those who heard it, but especially for those who were convinced by it and tried to internalize it. Finally, it was no piece of cake for Jesus, either. There was no half-hearted response to the teaching – one either loved it or hated it, and it could have real consequences for those who accepted it. In a very real sense, one's world ends when one chooses to follow Jesus.

Jesus' departure

Although the Gospel of Thomas contains no narrative relating Jesus' death, it does contain verses that suggest he will not always be among them. Jesus seems to imply this when he says, rather ominously, "Many times you wished to hear the words I am saying to you, and you have no one else to hear them from. But there will come days when you will look for me, and you will not find me."

In the biblical gospels, Jesus is possessed of a foreknowledge of his impending death. One could read the same foreknowledge into this verse, but it is not necessarily a prophecy. All of us have to go some time, and Jesus may simply have been referring to a natural, physical death he knows is waiting for him. Or, perhaps he sees that the political chess game his enemies are playing is about to reach its culmination. This verse is interesting for other reasons, however, regardless of how one reads it.

In the first part of this verse, ("Many times you wished to hear the words I am saying to you") Jesus seems to be saying that he is finally revealing teachings that he has been circumspect about previously. Since the verses in Thomas are not in any discernable chronological order, this is hard to verify or explain. The second part of this verse ("you have no one else to hear them from") seems to imply that they could get this same knowledge from someone else – were there anyone else around who shared his mystical vision.

Another verse that seems to speak of Jesus' impending demise is 59, where Jesus says, "Look to the living one while you are living, lest you die and then seek to see him, and find that you cannot." On the surface this appears to be a verse about Jesus. But "the living one" could just as easily be the Divine itself (a specious distinction, perhaps, for the mystically inclined). Either way, the meaning is clear – one must seek in this world in order to gain benefit in the next.

Some Gnostic groups taught a similar concept. They believed that human beings were not born with a soul, but that if they were to have anything left after death, they must grow a soul in this life. This view appears to be supported by verse 28, in which Jesus tells us,

> I stood to my feet in the midst of the world, and outwardly I appeared to them in the flesh. When I came upon them, they were all drunk, and I did not find any of them thirsty. And my soul grieved for the children of humanity, for their minds are blind, and they do not see. For they have come into the world empty, and they seek to leave it empty. But now they are drunk; when they sober up, they will have a change of heart.

Human beings come into the world empty of soul, without an enduring identity. But when they "sober up" and can attend to the portentious teaching Jesus is offering, they will turn around and find a substance to their spiritual lives that will endure, and indeed, survive death.

Jesus certainly knows he will be missed. The disciples are very concerned about who will lead them when he is gone. In verse 12, the disciples said to Jesus, "We know that you will leave us. Who will step up, who will lead us?" Jesus said to them, "Wherever you come from, you should go to James the righteous, for whom heaven and earth came into being."

James is Jesus' brother, whom we discussed in our introduction. This verse was probably a later insertion by Jewish Christians to safeguard the authority of James (and to reinforce their memory of how things actually happened in the history of the early church), and to refute the Pauline Christians who propped Peter up in their own histories as the one to whom Jesus' mantle was passed. It may also have served double-duty to refute the Gnostic assertion that Mary of Magdala was the recipient of Jesus' authority.

Thomas' Gospel takes no position as to the manner of Jesus' end, nor whether or not there was a resurrection. These do not appear to be important to Thomas Christians (although later books of the Thomas school affirm a resurrection of some kind). What *is* important in the Gospel of Thomas, however, is that though Jesus once walked with the disciples, they knew that he would not always do so. But the Thomas school was comforted by the fact that it had a record of his teachings – a record we still possess. And these were what the Thomas Christians most valued. For it is not Jesus that grants salvation in their philosophy. It is his teachings that are salvific.

Is Jesus man or God?

In this whole discussion of Jesus' ministry, I have deliberately avoided the Big Question that has plagued Christianity from its earliest days: Is Jesus just a man, or is he God? And if he *is* God, in what way is he divine? The Gospel of Thomas give us quite a unique perspective on this question.

Jesus said to his disciples,

> "Compare me with something and tell me what I resemble."
> Simon Peter answered him, "You are like a righteous angel."

> Matthew said to him, "You are like a wise philosopher."
> But Thomas gives him a very different answer: "Master, my mouth is completely incapable of saying what you are like" (13).

This verse reflects the two poles of opinion at the time that Thomas was being written down. Simon Peter appears to be voicing the opinion of those Christians who felt that Jesus had been "adopted" by God at his baptism, and had become a divine being – very much like an angel. (The notion of Jesus being wholly and completely God as John would assert later in his gospel would have seemed a complete heresy to almost all of Jesus' followers in the middle of the first century.) Notice that this position is put into the mouth of Peter, which is no doubt intentional as it represents the "high Christology" of the Pauline church who claim Peter as their first bishop.

The other pole, represented by Matthew, suggests that Jesus is simply a man like any other, a great philosopher, yes, but still just a man. These words are attributed to Matthew since the gospel that bears this name was originally written for the Jewish Christians and presents Jesus as a prophet.

These two views of Jesus were held in some tension in the early Christian communities. The debate really came to a head in the third century. The emperor Constantine was gambling on Christianity as a means to unite his troubled empire. Then, just as Christianity was beginning to be embraced by the empire, he found that the Christians themselves were deeply divided about many issues – and the question of Jesus' nature was chief among them. The priest Arius was the figurehead of those embracing a "low Christology" (Jesus is just a man) while Athanasius represented the "orthodox," "high Christology" position (Jesus is God). To put the matter to rest, unite the church, and get back to the task at hand (uniting the empire), Constantine called the great Council at Nicaea.

Today, we would call such a proceeding a kangaroo court. Athanasius had everyone's rapt attention, but when Arius got up to present his case, the orthodox bishops put their fingers in their ears so as not to pollute them with heresy – not exactly a fair hearing (Van de Weyer, 17).

It is further frightening to think that such an important matter of doctrine was decided upon to settle a political situation. Instead of discerning properly and prayerfully over time, these delegates were forced to make a decision quickly for the sake of the empire. The opinion finally produced at the council is also suspect in that a high Christology mirrors the hierarchy of the empire. As God is the Father of Jesus, and Jesus is King of the Universe, so the emperor reigns in his stead and with his authority. The emperor, wanting to affirm a clear top-down form of government was no doubt more in favor of this option than the more egalitarian Christology of Arius and his crew, whose Jesus arose from the masses rather than descending from the sky.

Amazingly, both positions can be argued from different verses in Thomas. In verse 15, Jesus says, "When you look upon the one who is not born of a woman, throw yourself on your face and worship him – for he is your father." This seems to suggest that Jesus is rebuking those who might be tempted to worship him as God, since Jesus was – by all accounts – born of a woman. Only one *not* "born of a woman" is worthy of worship, for only God is unborn, uncreated.

On the other hand, in verse 30, Jesus says, rather cryptically, "The place which has three gods, all is in god; in the place where there are one or two gods, I am there in it."

Some have taken this to be an oblique reference to the trinity, but this is probably a mistake. The trinity is a doctrine that would not be invented for at least another century, and there is certainly the possibility that it is a later interpolation by Trinitarian Christians. The key to this verse may lie in its structure. It appears to be patterned on the kind of parallelism found in much Hebrew poetry, such as the Psalms, where something is said, and then in the next line is said again in a different way. If this is true, Jesus appears to be saying that all possible gods people might worship are all "in God," and that he himself is "in God" as well. Jesus in this verse may in fact be affirming a kind of divinity for himself, but whether it is an exclusive claim is open to interpretation.

In contrast to these polemic responses, Thomas offers a third alternative: mystery. "My mouth is utterly unable to say what you are like," Thomas tells him. This could mean that Thomas does not know, but more is implied in this verse. It is not that Thomas does not know Jesus' nature, but that he is not able to describe it in words. He is certainly willing, but utterly incapable. The truth about Jesus, like most great truths, is ineffable.

Lao Tzu ran into the very same difficulty when trying to describe the Tao, "The Tao that can be described in words is not the eternal Tao," he tells us. The mystery of the Tao is too deep, too profound. Words are woefully inadequate for the task. A screwdriver is a fine tool until one tries to drive a nail with it. There are things that words can do and things that they can't. Describing Jesus is a task of the latter variety.

The result of this is a subtle critique of the other two positions. It shows up the arrogance of those on both sides of this argument who deign to know who – or perhaps what – Jesus is. Either position collapses the field of potentiality that surrounds him. Thomas, however, embraces the mystery, and leaves this field intact.

The perspective of Thomas' Jesus

With so many views of Jesus evident in the many gospels we have, it is impossible to know how the historical Jesus viewed himself. Though the Jesuses of Matthew, Mark, and Luke seem sometimes unclear of their natures, the Jesus of John is quite clear about who he is and why he is here. And the Jesus of John is all too willing to disclose this information – often at great length. The more mysterious Jesus of Thomas is more circumspect, however. In verse 91, his disciples say to him, "Tell us who you are, so that we may believe in you." But instead of simply telling them – because that would be too easy, or perhaps, too difficult a task for language to bear – he says to them, "You read the face of the heavens and the earth, and yet you did not recognize the one who was in your presence; and you do not know how to read the present moment."

Jesus is not alone in his hesitation to answer this question.

When Bodhidharma, the great Buddhist missionary to China made his case before Emperor Wu he was asked, "What is the highest meaning of the holy truths?" Bodhidharma replied, "Empty, without holiness."

The Emperor then asked him, "Who is facing me?"

Bodhidharma replied, "I don't know" (*Blue Cliff Record*, 1).

Like Bodhidharma, Jesus may have felt that his true identity was ineffable or even incomprehensible. Another possibility is that it simply does not matter who he is. Just as the Buddha told his disciples, "There may be gods, there may not be gods. Whether or not there are deities is unimportant," Jesus may have felt similarly. Jesus' divine status (or lack of same) is irrelevant. What matters is his *teaching*, and whether the disciples can apprehend the unitive message he is trying to get across.

There is no mention of a virgin birth, of miracles or healings, of the crucifixion or a resurrection in the Gospel of Thomas because none of these are important to the Thomas school. Jesus is not at all concerned that his disciples believe in him. But the disciples desperately want to point to Jesus, as if knowing Jesus' identity was the key to their own salvation – and we still suffer from this compulsion. But Jesus is not having any of it. Instead, he tries to direct their focus elsewhere. Their worship is not what he wants. Instead he wants them to see the world in a new way, to really see it as he sees it – as God sees it.

The Gospel of Thomas portrays Thomas as the only person who really understood Jesus' teaching – the only one of the disciples who really "got it." In verse thirteen, Jesus tells Thomas, "I am not your master, because you have drunk and become intoxicated from the bubbling spring which I have measured out."

Thomas has "drunk...from the bubbling spring" that Jesus has "measured out," meaning he has truly internalized Jesus' teachings, and in so doing has succeeded in gaining the same unitive vision Jesus has. Because of this, Jesus rebukes him for calling him "master," because as far as Jesus is concerned, anyone who sees as God sees is an equal, and through his teachings he is calling all of us to be his equals. This is the other way in which Thomas is his "twin," not by accident of birth alone, but by the felicity of the "second birth," enlightenment.

And, as this book makes clear, this is not a status afforded Thomas alone. As Jesus said in Verse 108, "Whoever drinks out of my mouth, he will become like me; I also will be as he is, and that which is hidden will be revealed to him." The Gospel of Thomas bids us all to become Jesus' twin.

So why not just come out and say all of this plainly? What's up with all the obliqueness? Jesus may have been cautious lest his followers (or someone else not so loyal to him) consider him heretical. While John's Jesus has no problem announcing to the world his divinity, any actual person saying such things was likely to be stoned for blasphemy. Instead of answering his disciples plainly about the exact nature of his divinity (or, again, lack of same) Jesus instead hopes that the disciples will discover the answer to their questions themselves by careful observation, by "learning to read the present moment." Fortunately, in our present day, we do not have to be so circumspect.

Following Jesus today

Little has changed after nearly 2000 years. People still differ in their opinions on this enigmatic teacher, Jesus. Even within the same Christian denominations wide varieties of opinions are held – the debate over who Jesus is far from over. The discovery of the Gospel of Thomas is a watershed event in religious scholarship, but it is not going to solve the "man vs. god" argument.

One thing that postmodernism teaches is that reality is subjective. It may be that each of the disciples saw Jesus differently, and the communities they began and the gospels they wrote may reflect equally valid perspectives. There is the possibility that they are all true. The spiritual process in the 21st century West is to choose that paradigm that seems the most likely or functional and to *work it*.

This flies in the face of much of Christian history where one deviates from the accepted orthodoxy at one's own eternal peril. Salvation for most Christians throughout the ages rose or fell on one's loyalty to the "correct" teaching and the Jesus it points to. Yet the Jesus of Thomas does not demand spiritual allegiance. Nor does he ask us to believe in him or even to have faith. Like the Buddha before him, we are invited to try out his system. If it works, then it is useful. If it doesn't work, then we should continue seeking. Everyone has to discern this for him- or herself.

Just as the Jesus of Thomas does not need our loyalty, he also does not need to be defined, explained, or even understood. There is a lot we can learn from this intentional ambiguity if we can learn to embrace it, but that is no small order.

We have a compulsion in the West to pick everything apart and explain it. Our modern, scientific inheritance values empirical evidence over all else, and we are loathe to invest in anything that cannot be duplicated in a laboratory or quantified with mathematical proofs. Even in religion, we are not immune to this tendency. We compile "systematic theologies" that explain every mystery of God as if it were a butterfly snagged in the wild, lightly killed, dissected, reassembled, pinned to a board, labeled, and displayed in a museum. We have very little tolerance for mystery.

Yet this is precisely what Thomas opts for: mystery. Ambiguity is always a tough sell, especially in matters of religion where people expect to find answers. Many of us spend thousands of dollars a year – and scores of hours of our time – on psychoanalysis because we cannot divine the mystery of who we are even to ourselves. And yet how can we expect to be able to know with certainty a man who lived two thousand years ago, in an alien culture, of whom we have no first-hand evidence?

This is the arrogance of religion, and like Thomas, we would do well to avoid it. Just like the rest of us, Jesus is a mystery. He has always been a mystery, and he shall always be a mystery. No church council, no confession of faith, no bishop or preacher can collapse that mystery into a quantifiable certainty.

We can, however, celebrate this mystery, entertain ideas about Jesus, new and old, and establish a relationship with the mystery that surrounds him – that *is* him.

The Gospel of Thomas simply holds wisdom out for any who

will accept it. It does not demand that we embrace any orthodoxy, nor abandon it. Those who believe that Jesus is God will find in the Gospel of Thomas an invitation to closer communion with that God. Those who believe that Jesus is just a man will find in this Gospel an invitation to a more enlightened way of living. But, in fact, the Gospel does not ask us to choose. It doesn't ask us to believe anything at all. It asks us only to *do* something, to try out a method, a *way of seeing*, and to see what happens.

For myself, I choose to hold to an agnostic view of most theological matters. As soon as I commit to a theological position, I collapse the field of metaphysical potentiality, and I am coerced into a defensive posture against every idea that does not square with the one I have committed to. The great tragedy of this is that I am no longer open to learning.

The Jesus of Thomas does not ask me to take a stand. I can embrace him as the profound mystery that he is, just as I seek to embrace the deep mystery that I am. This is far from an easy path, however. It is very tempting to take the easy way out, to take sides in this great theological battle that has been raging for two millennia. Thomas must have felt very much like the odd man out when he confessed that his "mouth is completely incapable of saying," what Jesus is like. It was not a popular position then, and it is not any more popular, now.

But Thomas harbors no illusions about this being an easy path. Indeed, following the Jesus of Thomas today means being bold enough to make our own way in the world, spiritually. It requires a certain degree of courage, a willingness to be a spiritual adventurer, spelunking the darkened corners of the spirit where others fear to tread. It also means embracing mystery, and having the spiritual humility to realize that we do not have all of the answers. And it also invites us to seek out those answers for ourselves.

The Thomas Christians believed that the answers they sought were not contained – nor containable – in any book. But by meditating on the sayings they collected and venerated, they believed they might be ushered into that ineffable mystery they so thirsted for. That same promise is held out to us today.

Exercises

1. **Answer Jesus' question** in verse 13, "Compare me to something **and tell me what I am like.**" But instead of mimicking Peter or Matthew or Thomas' answers, give your own. Perhaps you will use a metaphor, or perhaps you will make some kind of theological statement. The key is to be as truthful as you possibly can, and to best represent your ideas about Jesus. You might find that you have more than one answer to the question. That is fine, too! Write down every answer that is somehow true for you.

2. Take some time to meditate on the answers that have emerged. **Ask yourself honestly, are these answers that are true for you now**, or are they answers that were true for you at another time in your life? Are they what you really feel about Jesus, or do they represent ways you think you are *supposed* to understand Jesus?

3. Finally, **describe ways that you would like to understand Jesus**, even if these are scary. You may have been so wounded by churches that you don't want to have anything to do with Jesus at all, in which case this book might have been hard-going for you. That's okay, and bravo for making it this far. But the question is still valid, how do you want to *understand* Jesus? On the other hand, you may have very conventional understandings of Jesus and the idea of holding him in a different way is also scary. Lean into this scariness and do not run from it. Answer it honestly. No one will punish you for being honest, especially God, who already knows how you really feel.

4. **Begin a relationship with this new image of Jesus** that emerges. Go for a walk with him. If you like, talk to him. Tell him about whatever anger or fear has come up for you as you have read this book or worked on these exercises. Don't worry, he will not be threatened by anything you have to say. None of this is actually about *him*, after all, it's about *you*, and Jesus can take it. Pay attention to the feelings that emerge as you enter this new relationship, and whatever shifts occur as your relationship progresses.

5. **What kind of life is this Jesus inviting you to?** What images, fears, wounds, ideas is he asking you to let go of? What kind of ideas, images, and ways of living is he asking you to embrace? Can you do it? Will you?

Bibliography and Further Reading

Aryeh Kaplan. *Jewish Meditation: A Practical Guide*. New York: Shocken Books, 1985.

Aryeh Kaplan. *Meditation and Kabbalah*. York Beach, ME: Weiser, 1982.

Aryeh Kaplan. *Meditation and the Bible*. York Beach, ME: Weiser, 1988.

Barnstone, Willis and Marvin Meyer. *The Gnostic Bible*. Boston: Shambhala, 2006.

Bently Layton. *The Gnostic Scriptures*. Garden City, NY: Doubleday, 1987.

Finley, James. *Merton's Palace of Nowhere*. Notre Dame: Ave Maria Press,1978.

Gerd Lüdemann. *Heretics: The Other Side of Early Christianity*. Louisville, KY: Westminster/John Knox Press, 1995.

Gerd Lüdemann. *Opposition to Paul in Jewish Christianity*. Minneapolis: Fortress Press, 1989.

Hans-Joachim Schoeps. *Jewish Christianity: Factional Disputes in the Early Church*. Philadelphia: Fortress Press, 1969.

Hyman Maccoby. *The Mythmaker: Paul and the Invention of Christianity*. New York: Harper and Row, 1986.

John Dominic Crossan. *Jesus: A Revolutionary Biography*. San Francisco: HarperSanFrancisco, 1989.

John J. Collins. *The Apocalyptic Imagination*. New York: Crossroad, 1984.

Marcus J. Borg. *Jesus: A New Vision*. San Francisco: HarperSanFrancisco, 1984.

Merton, Thomas. *Zen and the Birds of Appetite*. New York: New Directions, 1968.

Robert W. Funk. *Honest to Jesus*. San Francisco: HarperSanFrancisc, 1996.

Stephen Batchelor, *The Awakening of the West*. Berkeley: Parallax Press, 1994.

Stephen J. Patterson, et al. *The Fifth Gospel*. Harrisburg, PA: Trinity Press International, 1998.

Stephen J. Patterson. *The Gospel of Thomas and Jesus*. Sonoma, CA: Polebridge Press, 1993.

Van de Weyer, Robert. *The Call to Heresy*. London: Lamp Press, 1990.

Watson, Burton. The Complete Works of Chuang Tzu. NY: Columbia, 1968.

Whitehead, Alfred North. *Religion in the Making*. NY: MacMillan, 1926.

Woodruff, Sue. *Meditations with Mechtild of Magdeburg*. Santa Fe: Bear and Co., 1982.

Yockey, James Francis, *Meditations with Nicholas of Cusa*. Santa Fe: Bear and Co., 1987.

O

is a symbol of the world,
of oneness and unity. O Books
explores the many paths of wholeness and spiritual understanding which
different traditions have developed down
the ages. It aims to bring this knowledge in
accessible form, to a general readership, providing practical spirituality to today's seekers.

For the full list of over 200 titles covering:
ACADEMIC/THEOLOGY • ANGELS • ASTROLOGY/
NUMEROLOGY • BIOGRAPHY/AUTOBIOGRAPHY
• BUDDHISM/ENLIGHTENMENT • BUSINESS/LEADERSHIP/
WISDOM • CELTIC/DRUID/PAGAN • CHANNELLING
• CHRISTIANITY; EARLY • CHRISTIANITY; TRADITIONAL
• CHRISTIANITY; PROGRESSIVE • CHRISTIANITY;
DEVOTIONAL • CHILDREN'S SPIRITUALITY • CHILDREN'S
BIBLE STORIES • CHILDREN'S BOARD/NOVELTY • CREATIVE
SPIRITUALITY • CURRENT AFFAIRS/RELIGIOUS • ECONOMY/
POLITICS/SUSTAINABILITY • ENVIRONMENT/EARTH
• FICTION • GODDESS/FEMININE • HEALTH/FITNESS
• HEALING/REIKI • HINDUISM/ADVAITA/VEDANTA
• HISTORY/ARCHAEOLOGY • HOLISTIC SPIRITUALITY
• INTERFAITH/ECUMENICAL • ISLAM/SUFISM
• JUDAISM/CHRISTIANITY • MEDITATION/PRAYER
• MYSTERY/PARANORMAL • MYSTICISM • MYTHS
• POETRY • RELATIONSHIPS/LOVE • RELIGION/
PHILOSOPHY • SCHOOL TITLES • SCIENCE/
RELIGION • SELF-HELP/PSYCHOLOGY
• SPIRITUAL SEARCH • WORLD
RELIGIONS/SCRIPTURES • YOGA

**Please visit our website,
www.O-books.net**